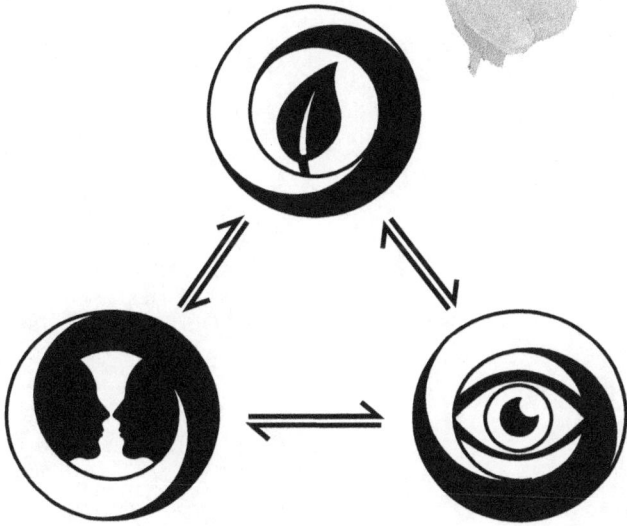

The supreme good of life is vitality.
And vitality is always seeping away.

Roberto Unger

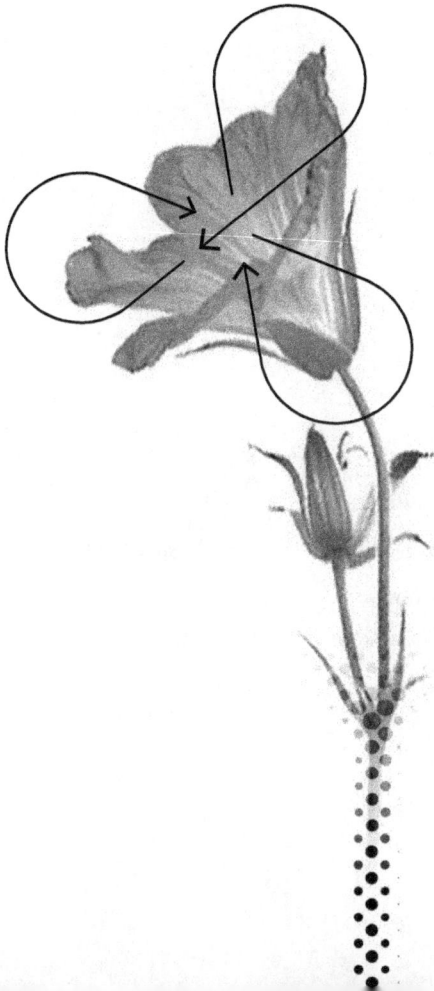

Author: Otto von Busch
Graphics by Otto von Busch & Calista Huynh

ISBN: 978-91-984047-3-9
New York: SelfPassage 2021

Second edition (March 2022)
Errors and omissions will be corrected in subsequent editions.

VISTAS OF VITALITY

METABOLISMS, CIRCULARITY, FASHION-*ABILITIES*

OTTO VON BUSCH

This book emerges from reflections around the time of the 2020/2021 lockdowns. Over the last years, a more general awareness has emerged around sustainability, environmental pollution, mass-extinction, labor rights and global injustices across the fashion industry. Climate change, toxic atmospheres, unpaid labor, cultural appropriation, social media burnout, you name it; the fashion system needs to amend its ways.

The common discourse around fashion and sustainability at the time of the lockdowns has seemed to gravitate towards the opportunity to reflect on our consumption habits. This is the time to clean up the act, a window of opportunity as the machine slows down to fix a system everyone agrees is broken.

Where the tone is not about patching up the industry to keep it running, the overall discourse seems to go into moralistic overdrive: look, we do just fine staying away from social events and never dressing up! Therefore fashion is unnecessary and vain! (again) Just dump it!

Too few questions are asked towards what *purpose* the system should be fixed. Before we fix it, perhaps we should think of what good fashion can do, and make sure we amplify these traits? Perhaps fashion should serve *life*, not the industry?

It comes down to this; think of fashion as the arrival of spring, an energy, a new light, the days grows longer, sprouts pushing up through the dirt, a challenge to face new adventures, a playful engagement with the pleasures of aliveness.

Let us celebrate fashion as a feeling of unfathomable depths.

CONTENTS

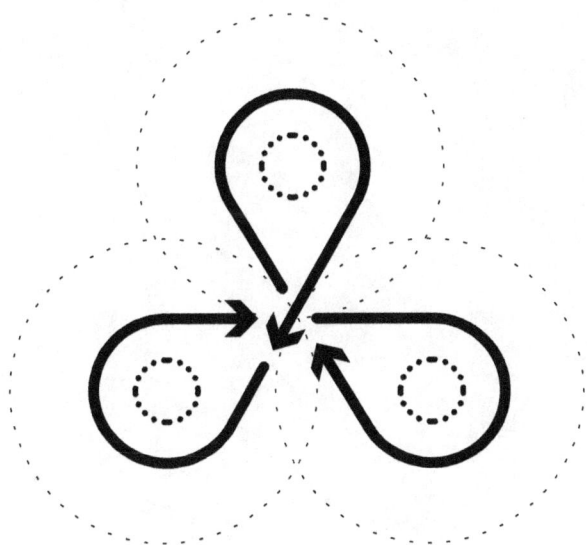

TOWARDS AN ECOLOGICAL
DESIGN INTELLIGENCE

Sustainable fashion is an oxymoron. The way we treat fashion across consumer societies is inherently unsustainable. As it exists under current economic models, *fashion plus time equals waste*. The very purpose of fashion is to be wasted. "If a person buys more than he wears," Roland Barthes (1983: 298) points out, "there is Fashion."

In the most common discussions around sustainable fashion, the purpose is to make the default settings of how we use and waste our goods less damaging to the planet. Default fashion is just that, a basic setting of habitual purchases. It may be satisfying but devoid of its full potential. Unfortunately, there seems to be little interest in changing much of the order of things or people's values and behaviors.

On a fundamental level, consumerism offers us non-commitment. We pay to use and then discard the trash without remorse. Consumerism is something like a one-night-stand. No hidden catch, no strings attached. It allows us to have free indulgent passions without carrying the risks of consequences.

When people say they want to make fashion sustainable, what do they mean? There are plenty of ways to make things last longer. A majority of the worldwide population practices sustainable behaviors, care for things, repair, and make do. No, what is usually mean is that *current consumption habits* are less damaging. Just patch up the default setting to keep the present system going.

This brings us to the present issue. One of the main problems with sustainability is that it sets the bar too low. Maintain the systemic norms, and we are good to go. There are few visions beyond making things bearable, manageable, and supportable. Even under circular business models, there are few visions beyond regenerating business. Keep on suffering, buy some comfort, keep going as long as the default setting doesn't collapse. It is a lazy approach to life, letting our time on earth waste away. We buy fast fashion now and push the costs to the future.

- "How was your day, honey?"
- "It was sustainable."

I think we can all agree the general sustainability discourse is misleading, if not miserable. It treats the default model of production, distribution, use, and waste as if it was the best we could think. As if today's default fashion is the utopia of dress.

The vision of *what fashion can be* must be more visionary than that. We need to practice better creative imagination. This book is trying to help us think about what fashion can be beyond the default working of things. It suggests fashion can be more vital than we think, and its purpose must be nothing less than to make us thrive as human beings, to engage in the splendor of passion and aliveness. If we think of fashion as a vital energy in our lives, then perhaps it can be worth trying to make it less impactful on the planet, our communities, and fellow organisms.

The most common definition of sustainability is to satisfy the needs and aspirations of today without diminishing the chances for future generations. As noted by deep ecologist Fritjof Capra (2005: xiii), this is nothing less than a "moral exhortation." It points out that we live beyond our resources and need to use our resources more equitably across the planet and across time. A green imperative is crucial for a healthy cohabitation on the earth. An inclusive perspective across all life and environments is undoubtedly needed to challenge what ecologist David Orr (1994: 2) calls the "industrial mind," the mindset prioritized across the economy. Yet, unfortunately, this moral calling can also cause problems. Too often, we encounter the idea that sustainability comes with awareness. We get lazy, thinking having awareness, or being "conscious" equals being sustainable. Unsustainable behavior thus gets laden with uncertainty, blame, and shame. It quickly devolves into a form of elitism between those who are enlightened and those who are depraved, or more so, those who can *own* or *afford* sustainable goods, and those who cannot. As John Ehrenfeld (2013) points out, we need another story, not just about satisfying habitual desires and needs in non-damaging ways, but that has a goal of life flourishing on Earth, to grow, develop and unfold.

A vitalist perspective in fashion starts the sustainability journey by affirming how fashion contributes to a sense of aliveness. Sustainable practice is not merely to keep living but to enhance life and desire. It stands as an alternative to the Victorian and moralistic discourse that blames the poor for wanting too much. It affirms fashion as a force contributing to human health and flourishing - we must start there. Less stuff should be wasted, fewer resources extracted, we should minimize pollution and suffering. But while we are anyway remodeling fashion, let us also make it more engaging. Let it make us become more fashion-*able*!

The focus on aliveness and fashion-abilities are tools to approach fashion and sustainability from a different angle. As I see it, a striving for ecological fashion-ability is in tune with Orr's (1994) call for an *ecological design intelligence*. This, he suggests,

> "is the capacity to understand the ecological context in which humans live, to recognize limits, and to get the scale of things right. It is the ability to calibrate human purposes and natural constraints and do so with grace and economy." (Orr 1994: 2)

There has been an emergence of ecological thinking across design over the last decades. While many industries have had policies and constraints imposed on them to mitigate pollution and waste, the fashion industry, to a large degree, has gotten away with consumer-driven awareness campaigns and minor fixes. If fashion is by definition a form of surplus and abundance, fashion needs a mindset attuned to its social and emotional purpose. It cannot simply optimize its way out of unsustainable practices. Fashion needs to *find its own* ecological design intelligence. It is a perspective that strives to keep the traits of fashion, abundance, excess and passion, in tune with the environmental constraints of our planet.

Design is how we shape the world according to human intentions. With fashion, it gets more complicated, as the intent gets entangled with desire and exuberance. Our ecological predicament needs industrial as well as spiritual changes. But it is far too easy to just call for raised awareness and morally correct behaviors and punish the passions. We need new figures of thought to make us flourish with fashion, thrive beyond the act of buying more stuff. Sustainability is not so much about solving a problem as much as *solving a pattern*, as Wendel Berry (1981) notes. Technology or economics will not fix it, and we must work from a more holistic pattern that lets passions and desires also fit without condemnations and hypocrisy.

With this book, a vitalist pattern is suggested to facilitate an ecological design intelligence attuned to fashion. This is no return to a mythic condition of ecological innocence, slowness, or wholesomeness, or that fashion should be done away with. Life itself is not necessarily slow. It moves in a multitude of overlapping paces and cycles. Seeking features from the processes that enhance the living potentials of the biosphere, the aim is to see how fashion can contribute to our sense of aliveness while also becoming more sustainable to the living environment on our planet. This aliveness should not be reduced to merely being positive, happy, or that certain practices are healing. As we will see further on, the vitality of aliveness is full of gambling, risk, and challenges. It also facilitates more convivial and imaginative flourishing intensities of passions, excitement, dopamine kicks, and presence in life. *If fashion is of any good, it must be vital, or it is nothing.*

So, what is meant by fashion throughout this text? "To dress like everyone else, but *before* everyone else," is a definition of fashion by Swedish fashion journalist Susanne Pagold that I work with. It places fashion in the everyday, in relation to the industry, but also amongst "everyone," a special everyone; *this*, not *that*, everyone else. It hints at motility, that fashion is in social motion. Not necessarily top-down, but in a direction aimed at with the "before." As will be seen throughout this book, this motility means putting oneself out there to *appear before others*, to be judged. It is a risky game, a challenge towards "everyone else." Think of it as a vulnerability that is played as a gamble, against ourselves as much as our peers, and it is this that makes fashion alive to us.

In this book, I will take you on a journey to explore fashion as a vital force to engage, play and direct in ways that trigger aliveness. In the first chapter, we will explore the basis for an *ecological design intelligence* emerging from the principles of living systems, aliveness, and feeling. With this outlook, we can think fashion beyond products and goods, challenging the industrial mind that saturated fashion thinking.

The second chapter opens a discussion on how we can question and rethink the *purpose* of fashion. If we are to mitigate issues of the fashion industry, we must think of what we want fashion to promote more than just selling more stuff. To create better practices, we must think of what good fashion can bring to our practical, social, and emotional life in the form of vital dynamics, desires, and feelings. The goal to amplify flourishing must guide the intentions of emerging design principles.

To place these intentions in a framework that can help further aliveness, the third chapter examines how fashion designers can move from thinking of addressing sustainability in isolation, to instead move towards intervening in the *patterns* of interlinked vital realms, or what we will call the *vistas of vitality*. These three domains are shaped by their own environments, by the elemental, relational, and imaginal energies that animate their specific niche.

The fourth part sets out to examine the living principles that animate and sustain the living *metabolism of fashion*. Fashion feeds on energies and matter in ways that assimilate the subject into their environment. These metabolisms cut across the vistas to shape their own patterns, but face the risks of undernourishing the metabolisms, causing deprivation, infarct, or shrinking the living system. In this case, aliveness is impeded, producing conditions of impoverishment. The other side is overfeeding the metabolism, overshooting the systemic carrying boundaries, which causes stress, pollution, and burnout.

The final chapter looks towards *fashion-abilities* as a tool to amplify and give users agency to shape and design their relationships with fashion, supported by services and experiences, or what we will call the *depth of engagement*. Fashion-abilities link material goods, services, and experiences with the capabilities, skills, and wisdom of being. The aim is to make fashion serve inner explorations and expand the user's sense of self-knowledge and aliveness.

As we will see, circular systems and metabolisms need their *balance*, and we need to recognize and work with these systemic patterns. To help develop these new patterns of metabolic systems, the last part of the book gives us a series of diagrams that opens up to reimagine the circulation of materials and energies in their vistas. They ask questions to help designers rethink how businesses operate between the three vistas. With these diagrams, a reader can start connecting and amplifying the living principles at work in each, searching for transversal processes and exchanges. To foster ecological design intelligence, we will need to find new ideas that promote vital fashions in the connections between the vistas. The hope is that a reader will leave the book with some of this work ready to be put into action, and with sketches ready for communicating with the team of collaborators .

There are several limitations to this creative inquiry. Grounding discussions in inherent properties of life is a tricky business. Nature is bound together by endless ecological connections and causal relationships. Too often, "nature" is used as an excuse for determining how things should be, such as a "natural order" of hierarchies or a "survival of the fittest" competitive environment. However, this text aims to use the properties of living systems as a mode to expand how we think things *could be*. Using life as a point, or more, a force of reference, the task ahead is to reimagine what fashion practice could be and how it can serve living processes. How it could make more people flourish and quench their thirst for pleasure and life. The task ahead is thus not primarily to understand nature right, but to enrich the soil of fashion practice, add nutrients to the designer's ways of working, and offer a prism through which to see a broader palette of options for developing new ways of thriving across the realms of dress.

Another limitation is the location of fashion culturally. Historically and globally, there are many ways to live and thrive. Many such ways do so without supporting the social phenomenon we may call fashion. And these are certainly also full of pleasure and laughter. The vitality discussed here is situated culturally in the West, shaped under liberalism and consumer societies. It is a setting that, at least in its ideology, promotes values of emotional development, personal growth, social mobility, civic liberties, and democratic ideals. A vital social life under such settings promotes dynamic social relationships, individual expressions, and a continuous renegotiation of social structures, traditions, boundaries, and taboos. It is in this context this discussion takes place, and the default settings of fashion will be renegotiated. There are undoubtedly many other ways to thrive, and fashion can work under many different arrangements, and I can make no claim on any universal principles.

There are certainly other limitations and mistakes of my own making. But I hope you, the reader, will find a creative lens through which to see potentials for new design practices that enhance feeling, desire, and aliveness, yet still keeps fashion healthily within planetary boundaries. It is a prism through which to see, think and seek, and practice new paths for fashion design.

> **Reflection:**
>
> Think of an everyday situation with fashion;
>
> - *Where* do you encounter fashion?
> - What *form* does it take?
> - When you *purchase* fashion, what do you buy?

Lust for life

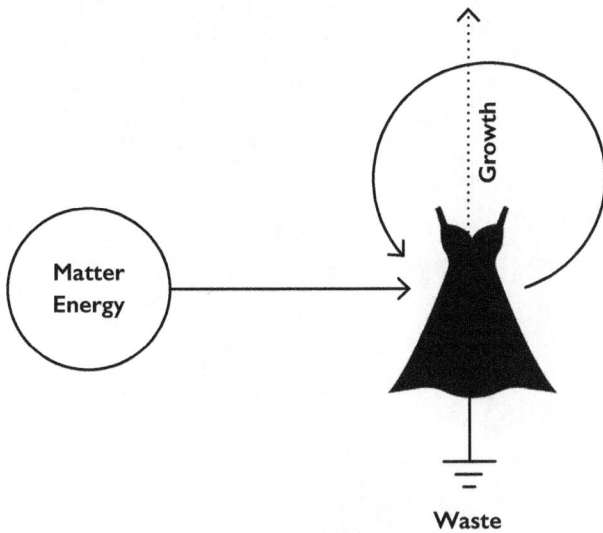

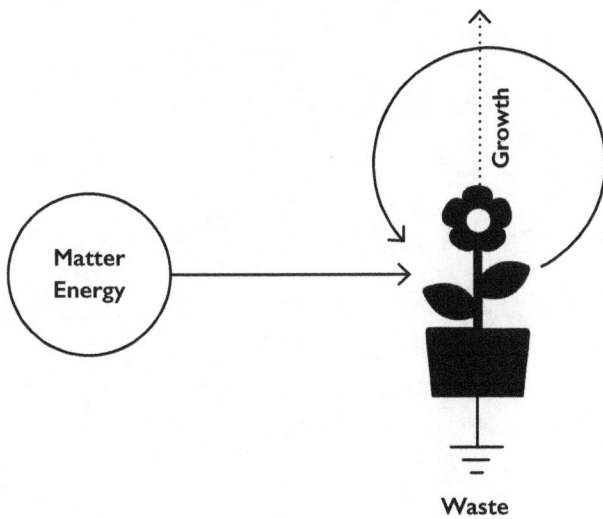

A VITALISM OF FASHION

When seeing someone looking fashionable, there is something in our attention that captures their look. Even if the person catching our attention may not having a confident attitude or express overt self-esteem, there is something that just seems *right*. Without a word, they just seem to *know*. They have taken a step into what comes ahead, and somehow we can all recognize fortune is on their side. They are not left drifting aimlessly in the currents of the moment, nor are they safely coasting downstream. We look at them, and we see that they are the pilots of their own destiny. And they steer their steps with a vital certainty.

To appear before others is to set oneself out into the chaos of unknown judgments. We seek to understand the currents for such an unsettling journey, align ourselves with the fates, and navigate long with the appropriate winds. We seek assurance our looks will work as we intend. We need faith that the journey across the social storms will not be a disaster. In this way, fashion joins many other forms of cosmetic practices. The word *cosmetics* derives from the Greek term κοσμητικὴ τέχνη ("kosmetikē tekhnē"), that is, the technique of ordering or arranging, as in ornamentation. The cosmetic is an orientation of appearance, to appear in a manner that speaks to how a culture or society arranges the laws and meanings of appearance and attraction. Like fashion, the cosmetic orients attention and practices between users and audiences. Social trajectories are drawn, anticipation builds up, a sense of direction is made manifest.

There is something about fashion that is different from clothes. Fashion is a shimmer of the now, but it is also more than a look or a style. Fashion has momentum. With a velocity or a force of fortitude, it breaks into the future. Fashion is an exciter. I may be reluctant at first, and think "I would never wear *that!*" But at the same time, a desire within that moment has awoken - a calling for a thrill. A new craving is aroused.

Fashion orders the desires beneath our appearance in continuously new ways, setting a fresh course towards the emerging horizon of anticipation. The claim fashion does in the future stipulates a certain excitement. There is a *current* in the current moment, a swirling flow of progression, and fashion taps into that. With a daring spirit, we throw ourselves into the moment, and here, enveloped by the updraft, a vital energy animates us. That new perspective on the future, that look, it calls me, invigorates me, and once in it, in the excitement of the moment, I *order an emerging world* beneath me. I become the aviatrix of my future.

There is something sad about how most of us habitually engage with fashion. We reduce it to a commodity, purchase new looks on routine, swath our judgments in shame and guilt. But fashion is a sense of *aliveness*; it can be nothing less. Yes, there are certainly elements of anxiety and conformity enveloped in this social phenomenon, but it is not what I am after here. We all need to dress, and by being forced to appear, we put ourselves out there and are judged by our looks. But while clothes are necessary, and our social environment may add peer pressure and the whip of conformity, it is the carrot I am after. If we are to make fashion more sustainable, we must set our course to what fashion is *at its best*. Fashion is the sugar sprinkled on top of the dreary diet of necessity. If I have dressed up and feel at my best, I experience excitation, and my body moves with a new sense of purpose and pleasure. Fashion must be nothing less than a spark of vitality. As fashion scholar Elizabeth Wissinger (2007: 258) points out, fashion is "a felt sense of vitality, aliveness, or engagement that takes no particular form, but taps into affective energy". When this look speaks of the moment, there is more than style or character at play. Now, I am ready to be seen, and when I put myself out there, I am prepared to be judged by my looks. Sparkling, full of life, the fruits of the future are within my reach.

Fashion is best understood as a vital energy that flows through the current moment. *Bodies are animated by fashion.* Excitement and anticipation promise something new. With fashion, you do not stand still; its purpose is not to petrify but to roll, ripple, and cascade.

Throughout nearly all of the day, and most of our lives, we live in our sensory world through clothes. It mediates our intentions and shapes our bodies, behaviors, emotions, and presence. But fashion situates clothes in time, a time shaped by social and emotional relations and aspirations. With it also comes projections of dreams and fantasies, how anticipation flows between bodies. Fashion is nothing less than the orchestration of attentive energies; a rhythm we share between bodies, enchanting us to move, dream and desire in concert. With fashion, we feel an erotic poetry that engages the whole sensorium of the self, articulating new suggestions of how we may live. When fashion works for me, my looks evoke and touch the attention of others. It opens room for an erotic endorsement, not reduced to just sexiness, but the pleasure at perceiving attraction. As someone gives me an affirming look or acknowledgment, I feel a rush of excitement, an abundance of affirmation overflows within, and pleasure streams through my body. My neurons fire, dopamine rushes: *I'm alive!*

The sense of aliveness intensified by fashion is an erotic poetry of our broader sensorium, attuning the senses towards others. We should not limit it to if something is sexy or not, but as popular thinker Alain de Botton suggests, "to pronounce a certain outfit 'sexy' is [...] to acknowledge that we are turned on by the philosophy of existence it represents." (de Botton 2012: 45) Fashion lives through the excitement in search of shared fantasies and desires, unknown pleasures, and erotic enchantments. Aliveness attunes to allure, temptation, anticipation, delight, growth, and fulfillment. *Aliveness feeds us,* our spirit as well as our flesh.

In many ways, all creative abundance is entangled with the erotic because it ties into the qualities of sensual signification. Artistic endeavors are essentially expressive. In them, the pleasure of life and its beauty is a form of seduction in itself. Thus, it would be a mistake to think that fashion would not also be a celebration of the frivolous, pleasing and unnecessary: it is sensory and vibratory. Like the other arts, fashion could thus be seen as a bodily intensification, "vibration, waves, oscillations, resonances affect living bodies, not for any higher purpose but for pleasure alone" (Grosz 2008: 33).

However, as most of us know, the current model fashion is not sustainable for our living environment and planet. There is an urgency to challenge and reinvent the industry's predominant business models. Much hope is put to the wide scope of circular business models that emphasize the classic principles of reduce, reuse, and recycle, to uphold flourishing markets that support people, profit, and the planet. In most cases, these new circular models build on the existing frameworks in the current industry. They emphasize the circulation of goods and set out to reduce the environmental impact of this material practice. It is a bit less extraction, paying living wages, promoting eco-materials, and recycling more. With material production and consumption in focus, these models simply aim to preserve the status quo but with fewer unwanted consequences. They fail to recognize that fashion can be much more than it is currently perceived. This book will argue that fashion is much more prosperous and plentiful than the current industrial system. There are so many more ways fashion can cultivate aliveness than churning out new goods.

But not only that. The current sustainability models based on reducing consumption have dire consequences across societies. In consumer societies, the access to cheap and on-trend garments, which we often call fast fashion, gets to bear the blame for the current unsustainable business models. While we envy the rich for their walk-in closets, the poor get the rap for fast fashion. Under the contemporary discourse of sustainability, the wealthy, with enlightened and virtuous values, moralize and blame the needy for aspiring to what the rich take for granted. Simultaneously, the strategies promoted to tackle consumption tend to favor the affluent; they are the ones who can buy quality, preserve their social standing, have pleasant memories and vintage accessories to be attached to. To those with nothing, even less shall be given.

If we seek the pleasures and desires of fashion, we may also encounter a more holistic perspective of the environment in which fashion takes place and lives. The purpose of this perspective is to emphasize the abundance of vital energies fashion taps into. A circularity of material goods will continuously live under the scarcity the economy produces within the boundaries of this planet. Under current economic models, there will always be a scarcity of property, production, and profits, however they are distributed. A more holistic view on fashion can help new practices grow and flourish that have less environmental impact and are not hampered by scarcity limits. The purpose here is to bring aliveness to the center of our understanding and practice of fashion.

In doing so, this book promotes a change of perspectives. Firstly, to see fashion as a phenomenon of vitality and aliveness. To see the full potential of fashion, we must put vitalism and aliveness at the center. The second point is to open a vista for how these vital energies flow in circular ways throughout what I will call the three domains of fashion; the environmental, relational, and imaginal vistas of fashion. And the third point is to shift our perspective from fashionable goods to how the vitality of fashion cultivates *fashion-abilities*, that is, capabilities to engage, embrace and modulate the aliveness of fashion. Fashionabilities help us see beyond commodities and the distribution of goods, instead of focusing on the flourishing of users; that fashion is a life-giving ability that designers can help people cultivate and grow with.

Seeing fashion through the lens of vitalism, thinking of fashion as an energy helps push the models of sustainable fashion beyond the scarcity of goods and the dependence on material waste in the process of fabrication. I explored this theme in my previous books *Vital Vogue* (2018) and *Feeling Fashion* (2018) by seeing fashion as a form of flirting and a risky play we engage in to connect with others. Building on these two books, the point here is to put aliveness in focus, which in many ways adds a more holistic perspective to the previous discussions. The point across all three titles is to suggest how designers can help expand the scope of fashion to embrace an abundance of processes, practices, and pleasures.

So what does this mean? If we conceive fashion as a streaming of life-affirmation between peers, we can think of it as pleasures that know no boundaries. If fashion is cultivated and grown as a vital energy, we must not think of it as limited to fashionable goods. Designers can give shape to the vitality of fashion, engage us with it in a multitude of ways, and make it radiate across our social realms as an abundance of life. As we move on, we will explore three different domains of vitalism in fashion and how designers can cultivate, tweak and redirect these energy flows to promote more sustainable and circular fashion practices. This is fashion: the shared sense of aliveness that surges through your body and into those whose attention you touch. As it flows between us, it is an emotional rush you cannot experience alone.

Vitalist biomimicry

Our planet is our home, and we share it with many other living organisms. Yet, we are not very good neighbors under the current working conditions. There has been plenty of reports on how the fashion industry contributed vastly to the deteriorating conditions of the planet. Over the last years, there have been some significant contributions to challenge the dominant paradigm in fashion. *The Earth Logic Fashion Action Research Plan* (2019), authored by fashion scholars Kate Fletcher and Mathilda Tham, offers a visionary trajectory to change fashion practices across the industry. The plan emphasizes how fashion designers and brands can move beyond the growth logic and towards operational models that stay within the planetary boundaries. Another report is *The Nature of Fashion: Moving towards a regenerative system* (2020) by the Biomimicry Institute, which suggests working guidelines towards regenerative agriculture and sustainable fibers that nourish rather than pollute the environment. These contributions offer helpful advice and visionary projections on how the principles of life on Earth can guide fashion design.

They are not alone. There is a rising interest in fashion practices that build upon the work of Cradle to Cradle and Circular Economy design principles and frameworks of Doughnut Economics, that also the approach I take here. The overarching point is to work under the guidelines that sustain the dynamic equilibrium of living systems that make up nature on Earth. Rather than merely follow profits and human user-friendliness, the point is to make sure the principles of nature act as banisters as much as limits to human industriousness.

So is this vitalist perspective on fashion a form of biomimicry a reader may ask. Biomimicry looks to nature to address design problems, such as replicating organic processes and structures to make systems more sustainable or enhance construction techniques and find lighter materials. In the realm of fashion, biomimicry is often expressed in the development of new organic and more sustainable materials or modifying the circulation of eco-friendly goods to replicate the regenerative processes of the natural environment. As it is popularly thought, biomimicry is a way to make design and engineering practices learn from nature and live according to its laws. This is a wholesome approach, and designers have a lot to learn from evolutionary processes and learning to stay within the boundaries of what our planet can support in the long run.

However, this book presents a perspective on fashion beyond biomimicry in many ways. Whereas biomimicry turns insights from the natural environment into workable principles for industrialism and consumerism, the purpose here is to turn the principles around. The aim is not to make clothes that are more "natural," and with these, we keep on being passive consumers of more eco-friendly goods. Instead, the purpose is to learn from living principles to change our behaviors towards living practices that are more livable, more thriving, more attuned to the passions of aliveness.

Furthermore, sustainability is not enough. If I ask how your day was and you tell me it was "sustainable," we would not necessarily interpret that as a good day. We need to set the aim higher. Fashion must be much more than sustainable; it should at least help us thrive, feel in control of our lives, relish in aliveness and human flourishing. Should we not cultivate a fashion that allows us to unfold a creative imagination, exuberant, intoxicating, and sparkling with spontaneous liveliness?

The purpose of the models suggested we will encounter further on is to push beyond biomimicry as primarily engaging with structures, processes, and materials of nature, towards what we could call this a *vitalist biomimicry*, a biomimicry of a nature of feelings. Here, the aim is to see nature not primarily as a wonder of engineering but as a poetic domain and amplifier of aliveness.

The aim of fashion must be nothing less than an aspiration for life, a force of life that helps the wearer to unfold its ambitions in life, to desire and propagate itself. This is the hunger that is life, and fashion shares this hunger for life. Aligning with the work of biologist Andreas Weber in his book *The Biology of Wonder* (2016), we can think of fashion as a tool for what he calls "poetic ecology."

> "It is poetic because it regards feeling and expression as necessary dimensions of the existential reality of organisms - not as epiphenomena, or as bias of the human observer, or as the ghost in the machine, but as aspects of the reality of living beings we cannot do without." (2016: 3)

From this viewpoint, Weber sees feelings and desires as the animating principles that guide life as organisms bring forth values and meanings, and these are "indispensable elements of a scientific description of life." (2016: 4) Poetic ecology is guided by what Weber calls the organic *Laws of Desire*. The First Law of Desire is that all living beings want more of life, making them necessarily bodies of feelings; they want more of that which means something. All living organisms are sensory beings, striving for positive valence, drawn as feeling bodies towards qualitative experiences. The Second Law of Desire is that the wish to live is expressed in the living body of each organism, not hidden within (for example, in genes or drives). The inner perspective corresponds to the external aesthetic reality of being. Meaning makes itself seen and manifest in the body and animated by the meaning of its desire. "The desire for life springs from hunger and thirst, and replenishes itself in growth and joy and thus becomes transparent in the body's gestures. Organisms, therefore, are not one-track machines. They are instruments of desire." (2016: 29) The Third Law of Desire posits the need for a being's mirroring in its environment, that the surrounding responds to the presence of life. "Only in the mirror of other life can we understand our own lives. Only in the eyes of the other can we become ourselves." (2016: 30) Life does not exist in a vacuum but evolves in relation to how its feelings and desires are mirrored back as meaningful. Biologist Humberto Maturana famously posits, "Living systems are cognitive systems, and living as a process is a process of cognition. This statement is valid for all organisms, with and without a nervous system." (Maturana & Varela 1980: 13)

It does not take much to draw parallels between Weber's Laws of Desire and fashion. Desire, feeling, mirroring, and a hunger for more life; yes, these principles are well attuned with an everyday fashion experience. With fashion, designers work to shape a phenomenon that is more than merely a symbol of vanity, class communication, or expression of lifestyle. There is something deeper and more affirmative going on, something that connects us to the basic principles of life that guide our desires, everyday strivings, and sense of aliveness. Fashion is attuned to the vital workings at the very basics of our lives.

This means we have more work to extend biomimicry in fashion beyond making eco-friendly materials and supporting regenerative agriculture. Making fashion sustainable is not enough. Fashion can become more vital, more life-affirming, more nourishing to us than merely consuming new goods: fashion must do nothing less than making us thrive in an abundance of vitality!

Reflection:

Think of an everyday experience with fashion;
+ When fashion works for you, *how do you know?*
+ When fashion works, *how does it feel?*

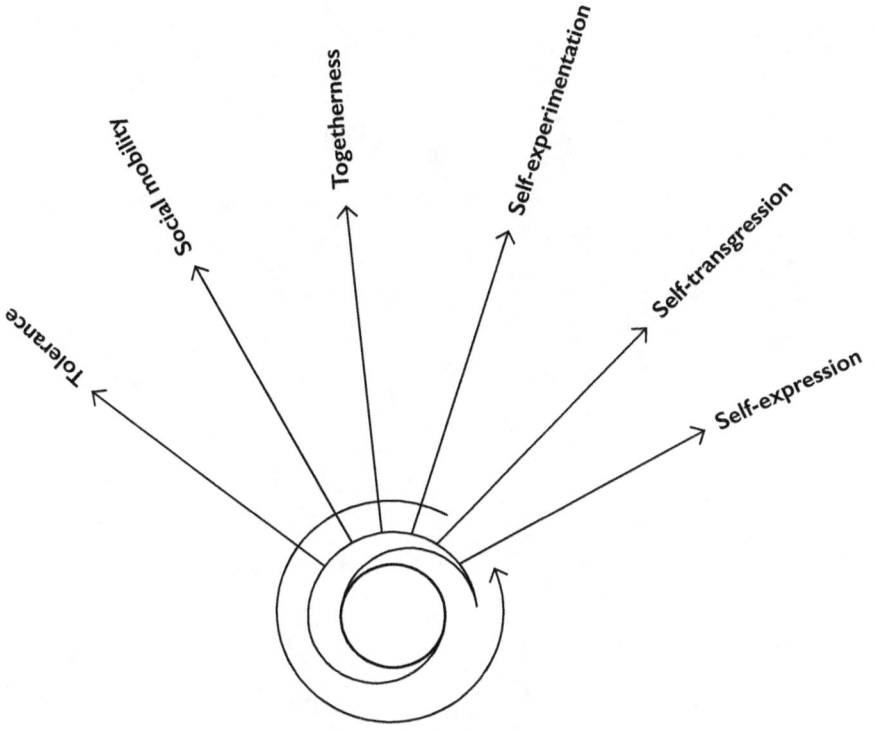

Tolerance

Social mobility

Togetherness

Self-experimentation

Self-transgression

Self-expression

THE VITAL PROMISE:
WHAT CAN FASHION DO?

Aliveness and vitalism may all sound good, but how can we relate this to the current workings of fashion? Let's take a step back to examine fashion in relation to society and see if we can think of how fashion may add to the vitality of social life.

On a fundamental level, we can start to think of clothing as a base necessity, like essential nutrients, while fashion acts as the sugar and sweets of pleasure on our diet. Here, the fashion designer is like the confectionery baker. On the one hand, the designer offers some bread for daily nutrition, but also some more sweet and exquisite desserts for special occasions. Yes, societies survive without sweets and bakeries, but we must also see that they serve a special function in making life pleasant. But yes, you are right, we can't live on cake alone.

Or we can think of the fashion designer as a florist, arranging flowers in ways that seduce the senses. Like the baker, the florist adds a sensibility to the world, even if cut flower arrangements are vain and unnecessary. The practice of the florist also highlights an issue with a material-based focus on sustainability: the flowers themselves may be biodegradable, yet the industry is not. Pesticides and transportation are polluting, and even local production has its issues. Think even of the gardener, and we find how entangled many biologically healthy practices are still producing waste and pollution.

Of course, neither the baker nor the florist is as wasteful as the fashion designer, yet their practices can be examples of how much of life takes place as a boost or exuberance of energy. As the French intellectual George Bataille (1991: 21) argues, life squanders excess energy.

> "The living organism, in a situation determined by the play of energy on the surface of the globe, ordinarily receives more energy than is necessary for maintaining life: the excess energy (wealth) can be used for the growth of a system (e.g., and organism); if the system can no longer grow, of it the excess cannot be completely absorbed in its growth, it must necessarily be lost without profit; it must be spent, willingly or not, gloriously or catastrophically."

Emerging from the superabundance of energy emerging from the infinite outpouring of energy from the sun, the practices born in this profound stream of excess is the life of sense-abilities. Expenditure is the "curse" of living processes, Bataille points out, and human societies organize the squandering of surplus in festivals, religion, luxury, and war. And to that, we should add the practices of the baker, florist, and fashion designer. Like other curators of luxurious abundance, they squander aesthetic energy, and in the process, they teach us sensibility.

We must think of fashion in the energy stream of excess, the luxury of the sun about to be squandered to produce an abundance of life. A fashion that does not seek life, incites dreams and desires, is merely "dead" matter. Fashion is a particular sensibility (or sugar) in the way that it opens up the social realm, a vector for passions, and a continuous negotiation of both freedom and autonomy. When asking what fashion *can do*, we can trace the laws of desire as guiding principles. Here, it can be helpful thinking fashion as a living system, and fashion is a vector by which we intensify our sense of aliveness. The question is, how is it done, and how can we design it better and more sustainably?

From the first Law of Desire, we know that all living beings desire more of life. Organisms seek growth. However, this does not mean all organisms keep on growing throughout their whole lifecycle, even if many do continue indeterminate growth until they reach the limits of their support systems. For most organisms, expansive growth happens in youth. Yet even mature organisms need a continuous flow of nutrients and desire more life and feelings. With fashion, this is expressed in how we can modify our looks as an aspirational vehicle. We seek more life, strive for acknowledgment and growth through the expressions that fashion makes possible. Employing self-expression is a matter of personal and social development, a living refusal to stay stagnant.

The Second Law of Desire is that the desire towards life is expressed in the living body, not hidden within. That is, we should put priority on tracing the hunger for life in its expression rather than seek to unmask a hidden agenda (such as selfish genes). Feelings are exposed in our behavior, not only trapped within. Once again, when it comes to fashion, we could quickly think that expression is the means we use to place the self in a social context and revealing aspirations. But we should also think beyond that. "*Life* is feeling. A cell is feeling expressed in bodily shape. Feeling is the immediate impression of being alive. It is being alive from the inside." (Weber 2017: 68) This happens as living beings regulate the flow of matter through their bodies or how their behaviors shape other organisms and the surrounding environment. Feelings shape the external world, not merely our inner domains. But embodiment is also more than expression. And similarly, fashion is more than expression. They are both ways to attune to and assimilate to an environment in relation to one's goals and desires. In doing so, they fuel a sense of place, shaping an environment by being situated in aliveness. With the striving for life, aliveness is an expression of existence in a future unfolding with the impetus towards flourishing.

The Third Law of Desire posits the need for a being's mirroring in its environment, that the surrounding responds to the presence of life. Like life, fashion does not exist in a vacuum but is by necessity a social phenomenon. Fashion connects. It is relational. When Weber suggests life needs mirroring, it means more than the hall of mirrors in the fashion stores or the selfies and likes on social media. But it also highlights how life attunes to the environment. Life reads and responds to the development across the habitat it lives in and practices life within. Thus the mirroring in the attention of other organisms, in one's family, community, or amongst "followers," expresses a deeply ingrained existential dimension.

So, all good, fashion connects well to and amplifies living processes. While this may be good news, it also hints at the environmental issues of overproduction and consumption. As the aliveness of fashion is currently mediated through consumer objects, it leads to the simple equation that buying more translates to more life. And while we may often experience that as we leave the store with our new purchases on a dopamine high, feeling on top of ourselves, it does not necessarily need to be engineered in such a way. We can think of ways to trigger aliveness that is not bound to material goods and ever-increasing volumes of freshly purchased items.

However, before we go there, let's start by unpacking how the dynamics of fashion may contribute to the vital energies across society, breaking through barriers and fuelling open-ended and adaptable social relationships.

The vital potentials of fashion

If we say that fashion attunes to aliveness, this means it is in the dynamic and adaptable ways rather than in the structure of cells and habitats. We find fashion as a principle of a superorganism, a protocol between living parts, rather than in the matter of fibers and textiles. By being in continuous change, in striving for a new life, fashion triggers many moving parts across society. These can be processes ranging from small developments in materials and techniques to global networks and production chains. But more than that, it is the social movement and energies that fashion brings to life that animates social life.

Continuous new fashions trigger changes on many levels, contributing to evolutionary dynamics. Fashion offers a context for the innovation in new materials. We must not underestimate the usefulness of fashion as a push for more comfort or better materials. The military use of waxed or rubberized trench coats, velcro, and other textile innovations are often emphasized. But on a historical level, many material novelties emerge from fashions, and not least new breathable fibers and stretch material, to more inclusive fits have become popular and accessible with the help of mass-disseminated fashions. As it moves in and out of its cycles, fashions push new relationships to the body, the elements, and the environment.

When it comes to the societal and social spheres, the more intangible potentials of fashion act on our lives. While not necessarily truthful, it is the everyday masquerade of fashion that allows us to do some fantastic things with dress. As wearers of a second skin that continuously changes its meaning, we are engaged in a dynamic theatre where intentions and meanings are under flux, giving us room and agency to assemble and co-author how we chose to appear before others. By stretching a bit of wiggle room between the truth about ourselves and the way we appear, fashion supplies a social lubricant for play. The mask brings us closer together. This is what cultural critic Gilles Lipovetsky (1994) argues is the prime potential of fashion; it greases the social world, adding wiggle room, reducing tensions through its pluralist principles. It stimulates us, *homo consumans*, to "take greater charge of our own lives, to assume more self-mastery, to achieve self-determination in relationships with others, to live more for ourselves." (1994: 148f) While living for ourselves is a claim of individualism, the self-mastery fashion suggests does not happen in isolation from others. In relation to others, it is played out in the dynamics of desire, between attraction, rivalry, and togetherness.

Precisely by being a masquerade with continuously changing colors, enriching the mirroring in life with the playfulness of the passions, fashion acts to realize a vigorous sense of freedom. It relentlessly becomes anew, inflicting a change in expression across the social field, whether people want it or not. This is not a static freedom, but one that keeps shuffling the social domain, seeking new life. By acting in relation to these changes, people can use fashion as a vehicle to become an author of one's life, over and over, and in each new case shape another sense of selfhood.

Spanning across social boundaries, fashion also acts as a means for flirting, as connection, as mutual expansion. Through the masquerade, a poor participant can appear as rich or the other way around. With fashion, a participant can escape one's predestined place in society, cutting across divisions that separate people. As pointed out by political theorist Joshua Miller (2005), there is a potential in fashion to promote democratic relationships essential for a thriving social environment. Furthermore, fashion can enact the pragmatic promise of democracy: that things can change, and a population can claim agency together to shape their shared destiny.

Even if it can preserve social distinctions, fashion is an unstable weather system spanning the social world is per se anti-conservative, anti-fate, casting expressions loose in the constantly changing winds. Let's have a closer look at the relational potentials fashion offers the social realm.

Firstly, on a societal scale, the masquerade fashion allows for *social mobility*. I can dress up in a skin that does not represent the identity I am born into, such as my class, ethnicity, or gender roles. I can move transversally through the social sphere. Utilizing our attraction and curiosity towards the new, I can flirt with someone beyond my community. I can use fashion to align with or move across social boundaries. I can present an aspirational self with the tokens I pursue to the possible peers at a job interview or to my date. With fashion, I can use my appearance to convince peers I am in control, that I am the master over the conditions of my life, and my social mobility is legitimate.

Secondly, when it works, fashion may foster *tolerance* as it exposes the vast mongrel reality of human differences and heterogeneous desires. It can help foster respect for differences and sympathy for the conditions and practices of others. The more used I become to see a wide variability of people and their expressions around me, the chance is I can accept and perhaps even embrace more of these deviations from what I see as the norm. In this way, the quotidian masquerade that fashion opens for us can facilitate a dynamic social environment. In a pluralistic world, experiencing such everyday differences can help remind us of the continuous changes across time and how similar we all are in our disparate ways.

A third potential is how fashion opens room for experiments in *togetherness*. By opening communication channels of similarities and differences, our looks can open, attract or help modulate social curiosities and connections. A small detail, worn by someone we may have thought of as an otherwise unimaginative person, may suddenly captivate us and open a space for connection. We may get interested in getting to know a person for how they mix and match their outfits or how they have adorned themselves in ways that draw our attention. When fashion works in this way, it brings about the excitement of flirting, a thrill that binds and entangles attentions and affects and pulls us closer together. Attention is aliveness, and as this is triggered, we may embrace life differently.

As a fourth potential, we can use fashion for *self-expression*. Here, we let the appearance of an unseen inner quality of our life and its values become visible to others. We can express unseen tastes, positions, and desires. With a change in expressions, signs, and meanings, fashion creates a continually altering palette of possibilities. With specific references connoting more permanent characteristics and others being fleeting, the assembly offers a rich palette of variables to play with. This can allow us to meet and attune to new people more easily. We can express aspirations and our thirst for life and affections, and it may add a sense of aesthetic excitement to a perhaps otherwise uniform everyday.

On a more psychological level, a fifth potential is that of *self-experimentation*. By continuous new circulation of looks, subjects can utilize fashion to break apart and transgress habituated self-formation. We can play with taboo, experiment with the boundaries between identities and power, from appearing within the safe walls of the home, to the community support and play of the club-milieu, to the presentation of self in the everyday. The changing references of fashion can be utilized for probing an emergent self-knowledge beyond that which is assigned to us. We can modulate self-esteem by seeking responses from peers, affirming, and amplifying a sense of self.

Even more radically, and a sixth potential, fashion offers room for *self-transgression*. Here, experimentation comes to challenge the conventional and inherited boundaries of selfhood. With its continual change, fashion is a vehicle that, with each new expression, offers a vector for infraction or breaking apart from dogma. As each new trend comes with its look and limitations, it opens a new frontier to test and transcend what one before considered impossible or forbidden.

As an attentive reader can notice, the potentials are numbered as a journey inwards. In each of these latter cases, fashion is neither shallow nor merely concerns appearances. It is about claiming agency to sculpt anew the inner person we are, guided by the laws of desire; to grow, feel, and mirror. Here, fashion comes to give shape to the feelings of life, allowing the user to claim increasing agency. Fashion "is an ambiguous but effective vector of human autonomy," Lipovetsky (1994: 9) notes, "even though it functions via the heteronomy of mass culture." Under a multitude of masks, fashion offers its wearers a glimpse of unfathomable depths and a vital light by which to probe and expose them.

At its best, we can feel the living potential of fashion when it works for us - the intensity of becoming anew, of touching the laws of desire. In many ways, what we feel is an engagement with the radical pragmatic potential of fashion. With its continuous impetus of change, fashion casts off the straightjacket of yesterday's conditions. When it works on us, we are not trapped *here*, under limited circumstances, but in the surging embodiment of being *there*, in the place of living aspiration. This potential must not be underestimated. In its continuous change, fashion can be a tool to break away from arrangements of life that seek to structure and diminish our hunger for life. It speaks to a thriving future rather than the past. This is the vital promise of fashion, its prophecy: mere humans can become almost godlike.

However, as good as they may be, the potentials of fashion are also easily corrupted, especially when they are bound to a limited interface of ready-to-wear products. As complex as the global production chains are, ready-to-wear garments are easily quantifiable and engineered. This is what has made the default model of fashion so successful. Commodities fit neatly into the economic models of mass production and retail. At a low and accessible price, the item of fashion has come to serve an increasing part of the population that, outside of inexpensive and on-trend consumption, otherwise has little agency to change the conditions of their existence. With immediate and user-friendly access, aspiration and beauty become tempting to purchase cheap, pushing the consequences into the future. If fashion offers a buyer a moment to feel in control of their lives, this is what is bought and sold just a click away.

Trapped in commodity form, it is not in the interest of brands to disseminate the potentials of fashion widely. Any brand wants to make sure *their* customers access the potentials their designers can manifest in their garments. In this way, the default model of fashion is a victim of its success: sharing the potentials would mean fewer sold items. Sure, you can express yourself any way you like, but this is the way you should look to be considered one of us. At the top, the industry seeks to limit social mobility with higher prices, heritage crafts, limited editions, and clamping down on copies. The potential for tolerance is held back by the proliferation of profitable delineations, judgments, and bias.

In the end, the masquerade has always been played out with an unjust distribution of means. But we must be conscious that there are real consequences in how the values designers promote come to play out. This becomes even more crucial for how the discourse and methods are set up and promoted to make default fashion more sustainable. Under slogans such as slowness, transparency, and authenticity, it condemns populations left outside to be unhealthy, vain, and inauthentic. The standard path to a more sustainable fashion business tends to hamper the potential fashion has as a social good and a tool towards aliveness. Under the default mode, sustainable fashion sets out to reduce the harmful impact on the biosphere while still serving the rich. But it fails to assist the populations that need the vital potentials for fashion the most.

Expanding the perspective on fashion can help us see more avenues and interfaces towards cultivating and disseminating the vital potentials of fashion. But to do so, we need to move beyond the default mode of thinking fashion primarily as commodities. We need to look at fashion as serving a more intense sense of aliveness than merely accumulating stuff.

Reflection:

Global Fashion Agenda suggests "7 Things You As A Can Do As A Citizen To Contribute To Circular Fashion," and these are:

1. Treasure what you own to extend the longevity of your clothing
2. Borrow don't buy – if you need something for a one-off occasion rent it or borrow from a friend
3. Resell clothes so they get a second life (a resold dress reduces its CO_2 impact by 79%)
4. Repair clothes if they break
5. Recycle garments beyond repair – do not throw them out!
6. Shop less and buy smarter by shopping vintage, second-hand and ethical
7. Make it last – invest in high quality and timeless pieces

Reflect on the points above.
* What are the differences between the approaches?
* Which of these advice works out as well for the poor as for the rich?
* Are there ways to follow the advice and still get the thrill of fashion?

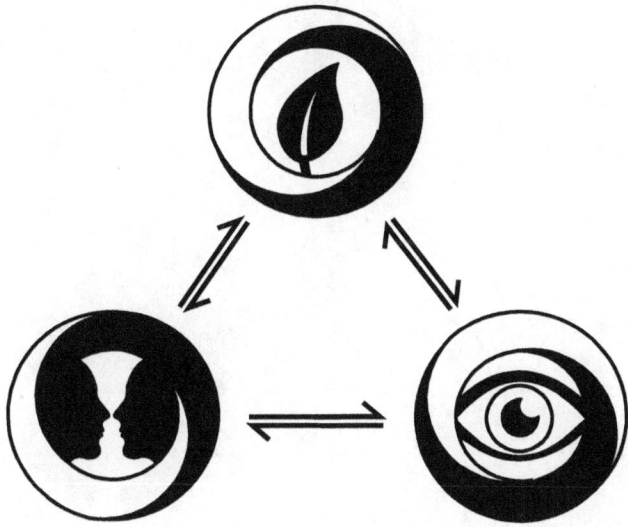

THE THREE VISTAS OF FASHION

Every living organism strives for life, to self-organize, self-reproduce, and evolve. A plant seeks light, to grow, to thrive. In biology, this process is called *autopoiesis*. *Auto* refers to the self and the autonomy of self-organization, and *poiesis* means making. Autopoiesis means "self-making," but as we will see more further on, we could also translate the term to something like "self-design."

It is easy to think of fashion as a purely cultural phenomenon; it seems reserved to the human world. Or even more so, it appears to us as a product of a specific form of consumerism, tied to the moneyed world, to capitalism, or glitzy celebrity parties. But new opportunities open when we think of fashion in relation to life, or the processes that bring molecules to organize, become energized, and start to *feel*. How do we think of fashion as an animating principle or a force that helps users to also seek light, to grow, to evolve, and to self-design?

It is its life-giving processes that propel fashion to such a powerful force across consumer society. Fashion taps into autopoietic desires in our lives and becomes a vehicle for our self-sustaining practices. Or even more so, fashion connects to our desires to grow, evolve, and self-design. And it does so in many dimensions, beyond the material commodities.

The vistas of vitality

Seeing fashion as a vital force or an animating principle of societies, lives, and desires, opens new possibilities for fashion practices. Fashion is energy. And energies can be manipulated, redirected, or inten-sified.

To think of fashion as an energy may not be as foreign as it might first appear. The textile fibers emerge from the processes of life. From the plants and organic substances in cotton or silk, to the millen-nia-old photosynthesis that makes up the molecules in oil-based fibers. But even more so, in social relations and our emotional lives, the energy flows between us, and we can trace its paths throughout our everyday.

Following these animating energies will make us recognize the more diverse realities of fashion, and we will see the flows through many domains. While production chains, goods, and services are easier to follow, social energies and desires are harder to measure. Yet, we can trace how fashion has real consequences and examine its impact at these places. That is, we can structure the framework around realms of fashion, or *vistas of vitality*, stretching from the environment over social relations and shared experiences of collective imagination to the dreams and desires of individual subjects.

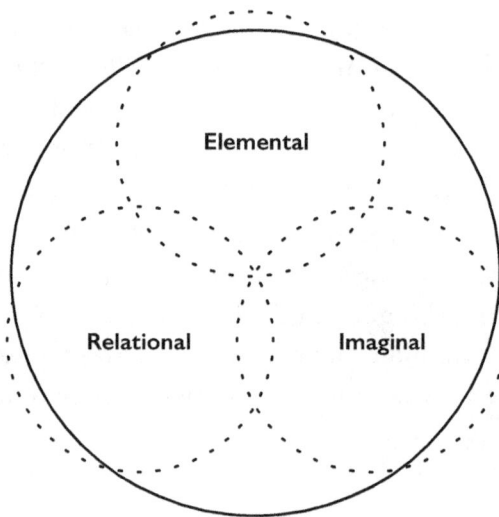

The three vistas as a consubstantial figure of fashion

We will place fashion in three vistas, or dimensions, of reality. They are the *elemental, relational,* and *imaginal* realms of fashion. Fashion flows throughout each of these three vistas, but in each domain in a different speed and intensity, and with varying consistency. In the elemental vista, fashion takes the material form of physical garments circulating through industrial supply chains, production, and use cycles. In the relational vista, fashion is less concrete and circulates amongst us as signs and symbols that guide social practices, hierarchies, and notions of status. Fashion circulates as ideas and desires in the imaginal vista, giving shape to our fantasies, projections, and figures of thought. Each vista exhibits its vital dynamics and metabolisms, yet they all intersect. We will go more in-depth as we move along.

Placing fashion in three different domains of reality expands the scope of how to pin down what we mean by fashion and how to manipulate its workings. This width of realities multiplies the vistas where designers can intervene and address fashion differently. With an extended conception and articulation of how and where fashion operates in our lives, designers have an opportunity to think more holistically of how to best address the issues fashion sets in motion in the world. This shift of attention towards a richer conception of fashion will also imply we can no longer primarily think of fashion merely as a product, ready-to-wear garment, or accessory. Neither should we limit our understanding of fashion as a semiotic symbol for communication. Fashion takes place in all three vistas, in some cases more intensely in one domain than in another. A more accurate figure of thought is to translate fashion to connote various manifestations of energy, from high density, in matter, to be displayed in more fleeting ways as emotions and passions. Think of it like this: fashion is more than atoms and particles. Think of it also as waves, rays, atmospheres, and emotions.

But more than an academic assignment of curiosity, what does this change apply, one may ask. Why all this mess for saying the obvious that fashion is something else than the latest bleached jeans and hyped t-shirt I am wearing? Like so many other theoretical endeavors, the purpose is to help articulate tools and models of thought for fashion practitioners to describe the environment in which they work more accurately. Having sharp theoretical tools allows one to work with and communicate with others how one works and what needs our shared attention. Articulation shapes our awareness of details, while it can also help frame patterns while also paint abstract ambiance. Models of thought attune our attention to what matters and make things visible and discussable, which allows us to change things. New models of thought help place us in a changing reality where previous understandings seem misplaced or have been undermined.

But first, let us first begin unpacking if fashion is something to pay attention to at all - and in such case, how, and why?

Three vistas - an expanded model of fashion

To think of fashion as more than a product may not appear too much of a task. Just visit a store, and we know most brands also put special attention to imagery, lights, smells, music, and the whole brand experience to make sure we purchase their goods. If we turn to how fashion education is expressed or how brands operate and retail is organized, the challenge comes before us as more profound. The industrial model of fashion is built upon the design, production, promotion, and distribution of fashionable goods and commodities. As the industry sets out to amend its ways environmentally, and shift along with online shopping, the immediate solution is to patch up the current working model and make it less environmentally damaging and push for experiences. But the goods still hold the center.

For sustainability, reducing the impact of material garments is a good start, yet it does little to change the pollution fashion brings in its periphery. This stretches from the pollution in logistics and packaging, chemicals used, and microplastics released in washing and wear, to the energy use in resale, recycling, and reproduction. Even if the goods themselves would turn out to be all-virtuous with zero footprint, the chain of events fashion commodities set in motion across the environment largely stays unsustainable. A more holistic approach is undoubtedly needed.

But we still have many other issues to address, such as labor, beauty standards, global injustices, and colonial baggage, cultural appropriation and exploitation, and much more. Seen in the bigger picture, the environmental aspects centered around garments are just one part of the many troubles fashion keeps stirring.

If sustainability in fashion means more than simply patching up the most urgent scandal and mitigating the most blatant environmental impact, designers and managers need to work across the broader spectrum of where fashion operates and not merely on a material level. This is where the three vistas of fashion come in, to help open an ecological design intelligence of how to broaden practices that cultivate flourishing through fashion.

Tracing the vistas of fashion

Framing fashion around three vistas helps put our attention to new things. Thus, the conceptual model of the vistas is best understood as a knowledge strategy. Its task is to show how fashion operates in ecologies beyond the narrow scope of the environment, or what we call nature. The aim is to expose the ecological and interdisciplinary vistas of fashion. While ecological and bio-materials are significant steps, we must also see sustainability within much richer scopes of reality. As pointed to earlier, the reason is that it is not enough to mitigate the pollution in the environment without taking into account the pollution that fashion contributes to in the larger realms of life. Whereas the environment is one of the three vistas, the purpose of the model is to help show how the three domains of fashion are interlinked.

The three vistas are the elemental, relational, and imaginal domains of fashion. The *elemental vista* denotes the material aspects of clothing, the textile that exposes or shields our bodies from the elements. This is a domain of fibers and materials, production technologies and recycling, factories and retailers, cotton and oil. Here, fashion is shaped primarily by atoms, particles, and matter. The *relational vista* is where fashion acts to take part in social hierarchies, identity production, semiotics, and communication. This most often emerges from material goods, but this is also a realm where simulation, simulacra, and ironic play with images and artistic and creative strategies take place. It is a world of hype, decrees, and influencers act in a polyphonic buzz, or where people are excluded or bullied for what they wear. In this realm, we can think of fashion more as waves of imitation and distinction, as energies rippling through the social organism of human relations. Finally, the *imaginal vista* is the domain of mental projections and psychological interactions. This is where fashion connects to fantasies and desires. Here, fashion affects self-knowledge and self-esteem, where our sense of self, or self-image, plays along with our projections and imaginations, and emotions. Here, fashion exists to us as figures of thought, as a mirage, or as fervent desires and excitement.

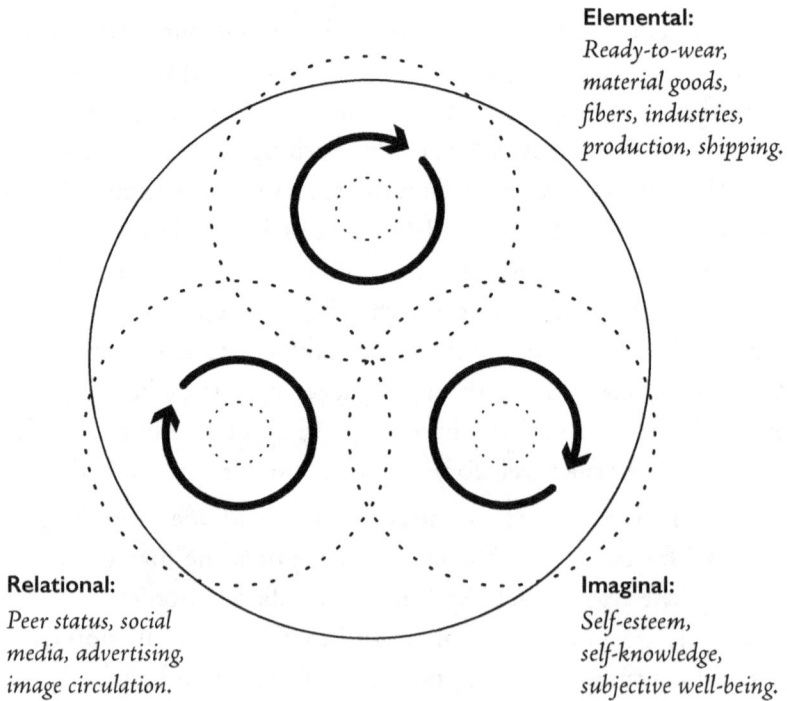

Elemental:
Ready-to-wear, material goods, fibers, industries, production, shipping.

Relational:
Peer status, social media, advertising, image circulation.

Imaginal:
Self-esteem, self-knowledge, subjective well-being.

The three vistas overlap with Felix Guattari's (2000) notion of the "three ecologies," which he frames as the environmental, social, mental ecologies. Following the work of Gregory Bateson's *Steps to an Ecology of Mind* (1972), Guattari points to the interconnectedness of the ecologies; ecological sensibilities are needed to address more holistic approaches to our world. While Bateson's and Guattari's work are central to the thesis suggested in this work, the emphasis of the three vistas is slightly different. Along similar lines, the Textile, Environment, Design research group at Chelsea College of the Arts has made a guide of three ecologies, built on Materials, Models, and Mindsets as a framework for sustainable material innovation, new business models, and a change in practices of care (Earley 2019).

The three vistas are similar to the ecologies above, but here, the purpose is to put our attention to the energies of fashion. As fashion is highly dependent on social hierarchies and the projection of desire, the three domains suggest a slightly different "slicing" of the ecological worlds seen through the lens of fashion. The elemental vista corresponds to Guattari's environment, the relational vista to the social ecology, and the imaginal vista to human subjectivity. In each vista, fashion interfaces processes that are present in that domain; the elements in the environment, relationships in the social ecology, and imaginal figures that animate human subjectivity. But again, think of these environments as only framed by membranes, letting energies pass through, and each vista animated by aliveness.

Follow the footprints

As a reader might notice, it is hard to draw distinct borders between the vistas, as they seem to overlap a great deal. Fashion spans all three of them, and a fashionable product has a presence in all three domains simultaneously, even if this presence is not equally distributed. A freshly dropped sneaker is, of course, a material shoe. Still, it also exists as an image or advertising object in the social domain, in comparison to other sneakers and users, and as it does so, it also manifests itself as something we may think of and desire; we may even be able to see an inner image to our mind of ourselves wearing the sneakers.

The sneaker exists in all three domains, but its presence is expressed in distinct ways between the realms and touches and affects our lives differently. The material aspects of the sneaker have properties that affect my feet. It keeps them protected from the elements, it supports my body for every step I take, and the sole of the shoe leaves distinct footprints in the environment. Let the footprints stay a little while in your mind's eye. These tracks are also an apt image of the environmental footprint the shoes leave; from the extraction of the resources in oil rigs and cotton fields, to pollution in its production and waste, and the labor tied to these processes. In the world of the elements, the sneakers leave material footprints. We can trace their physical marks on the environment in pigments in polluted rivers, pesticides in the air, blisters on the hands of workers. The footprints are more apparent in some milieus, like in the soft ground. We can see the mountains of waste, the overpacked warehouses of recycled clothes. Some are more hidden, like the pollution that happens in the extraction of

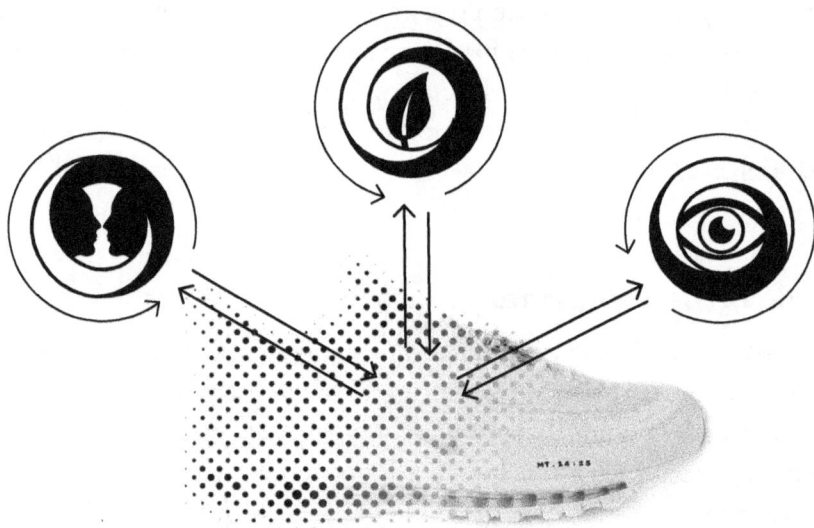

A garment or accessory circulates as substance in each vista.
The impact and density varies between cases and situations.

materials or the pipelines and refineries of the oil industry. Other marks are barely visible, like the contaminants from chemicals, the microplastics in the oceans, and fumes in the atmosphere. But everywhere they pass, the sneakers leave traces.

We can also think of how the sneakers leave footprints through the social world of human relations. Here, the sneakers leave a mark on our shared social world. We see these sneakers in images and ads, movies, and on the feet of celebrities. But they also live an active life in the interpersonal relationships I share with my peers. For example, I may share an interest in sneakers with friends, and I saw the latest drop of sneakers in my feed. There has been some buzz lately, something in the current social mood that just seems right in relation to these shoes. I can sense this new pair will be the next thing, and I rush to make sure I get in line. As I lay my hands on them, I consider saving them for resale, as I know this pair may be hot on the forums. Even so, I choose to use them, just to get some cred amongst some of my sneakerhead friends. And rightly so, my new sneakers leave some footprints in our community as my peers now start to ask for my opinion on some of these matters. Some new followers indicate my strategy also got adequate approval in my social media feed.

The sneakers also have a presence in my mental environment, in my emotional life. My daydreams and fantasies, judgments, and frames of reference are affected by what captures my attention. I come to see the world through the lens of fashion; what I consider to be beautiful or of prestige, and it also affects my sense of self-worth and my moods. Perhaps I was a bit down before, and I had a feeling this new drop could be worthwhile pursuing. In this case, they gave my confidence a boost, but the purchase also covers up that a rival had stepped on my esteem in one of the discussion boards on the topic some weeks ago. I needed to prove myself. Thinking of it, these new sneakers actually take up quite a bit of room in my attention these last few days, as I have been browsing around, getting a sense of what some people overseas expect from this drop. Suddenly, I feel quite a bit of my self-esteem is now tied to these sneakers. But I shouldn't worry too much; there will be new drops coming.

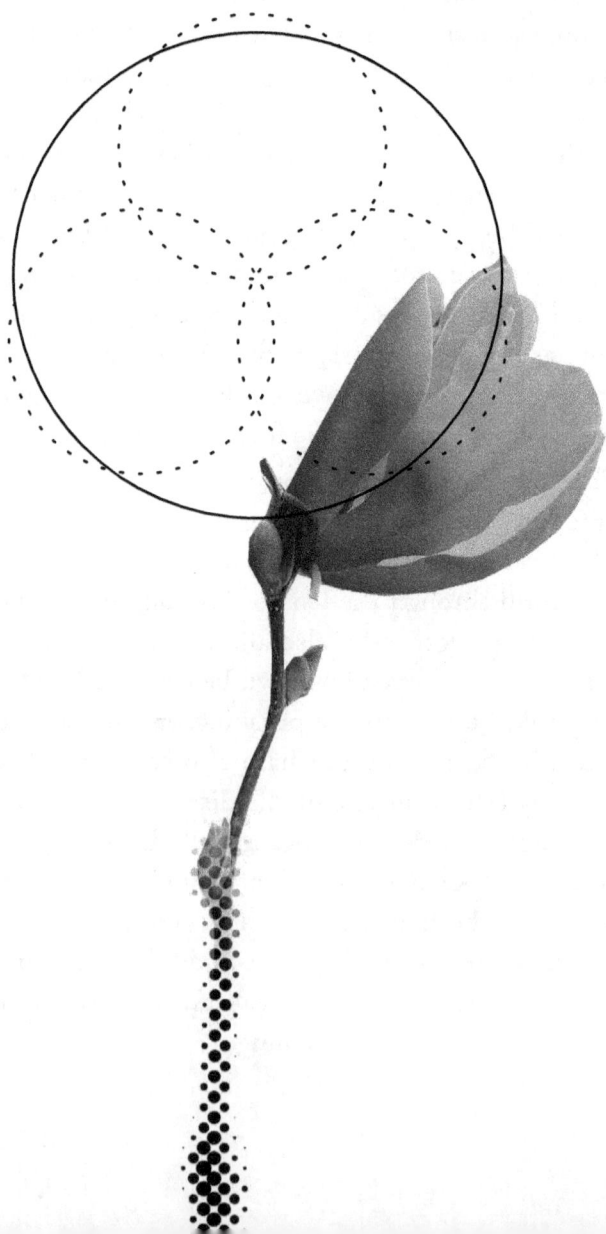

Reflection:

Think of one of your favorite garments or accessories, and ask yourself;

+ How is this garment *expressed* in the three vistas?
+ How is it *encountered* in each vista?
+ What kind of *traces* does it leave in each vista?
+ How do *others* notice these traces?

Multitudes

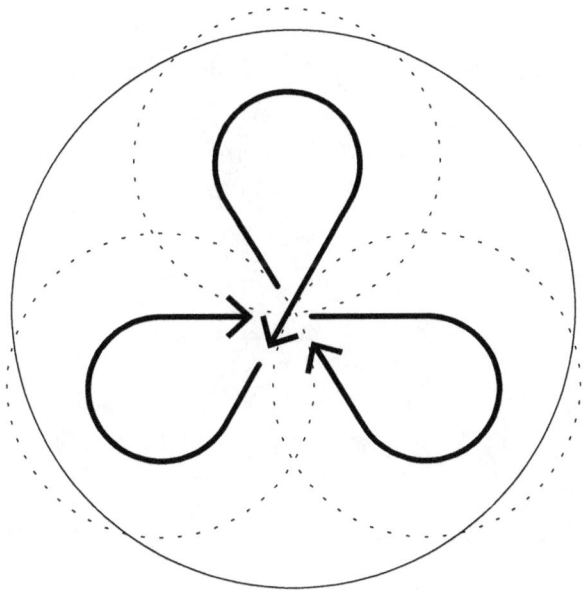

FASHION'S METABOLIC CYCLES

Fashion is always becoming anew. It is easy to think the essence of fashion would thus be change, but it is a specific change; fashion is a change in energy. The change we associate with fashion is an *energetic charge* that animates and intensifies life. So thinking fashion as a form of energetic flow may not be all foreign. The task is tracing and modulating the motility fashion animates across the three vistas to get the most aliveness out of it, yet with the most negligible environmental impact. It requires us to think more expansive, and together with the three vistas, thinking fashion as energy can help us think beyond products.

Seeing fashion as flowing across three vistas emphasizes how the material aspects of fashion are tied to social relations and desires in cycles and speeds. Change happens at different paces, and not necessarily in sync. As an industrial system of mass production, fashion thrives in the fast changes of seasonal desires, which triggers new purchases of material commodities. The cycles of production, acquisition, use, and expenditure of garments are popularly called their *metabolism*, likened to the life-sustaining processes that uphold an organism. Taken from biology, the term describes the transformation and expenditure of energy to maintain the conditions of life, in usage during a specific activity or over a lifecycle.

One of the primary advantages with the perspective metabolism brings with it, is that our attention is raised to see how the lifecycles of garments differ between the vistas. Not everything moves fast or slow, or in sync, and a significant challenge in making fashion more sustainable is to attune these cycles better to each other. A garment's material resilience should match its social and emotional durability so that a garment only used a few times does not spend decades later as landfill. And similarly, a garment that is meant to last must also be supported by systems and services that enhance its chances of longevity.

Fashion scholars such as Kate Fletcher, Lynda Grose, and Mathilda Tham have frequently used the idea of metabolism as a lens to understand the use and life cycle of garments. In Fletcher and Tham's (2004: 268) definition, a garment's metabolism connotes "the relative pace at which the garment is consumed". This points to how long a garment stays "fresh" and in use, and puts our attention on how garments are not only used on bodies, but stored in wardrobes and attics. A garment's practical use is not necessarily tied to the durability of its material properties. Different clothes are "consumed" in different ways as they pass through our lives. Fletcher (2018: 24) expands the definition;

> "Metabolism is the set of processes that occur within a fashion activity or entity in order to maintain its functioning. These include the transport of material assets between or around it and their conversion into fashion experiences. Fibre, garments, ways of dressing, use practices, etc. enable action by both expending fashion resources and building them up."

Fletcher's definition points to how many aspects of a garment's production and use that is in place to create the functioning that leads to a fashion experience. While the definition remains quite vague, Fletcher points to a depth and complexity of how matter and logistics support and enables fashion as an episode and situation we *experience*. In the end, a material metabolism is working in tandem with *fashion as a feeling*. This opens the use of the concept of metabolism to describe more in detail how fashion animates, energizes, and sustains the more existential conditions of our lives.

So what is a metabolic process? To turn food into energy, the metabolic system supports catabolic processes. They break down compounds and molecules to be digested and turned into life-supporting substances. The cycle also includes excreting metabolic waste, surplus from the life-sustaining process that can be toxic to the organism. It may be easy to think of metabolism as a sort of motor. With this metaphor, the metabolic process is like a combustion engine, with fuel (nutrients or sugar) consumed and burned to make energy, which produces motility. The emission is the left-overs waste. As compelling as the motor's figure is, organic metabolism is fundamentally different from the combustion engine. "Metabolism means tearing down one's own physical substance and building it anew with what comes from the world," Weber points out. "Metabolism means sharing one's own matter, and hence a part of one's own identity, with the world." (2016: 60)

> "In contrast to an object or a machine, a body regularly splits off a part of itself in order to survive and incorporates a piece of the foreign world into itself. This is precisely why it is wrong to compare a life-form with a machine: A machine does not metabolize. The fuel that I put into the tank burns but does not transform itself into another body." (Weber 2017: 57)

While the engine merely burns fuel while keeping the engine intact, metabolic processes make the food part of the organism. The waste from a metabolic process is scraps from the organism's continuously renewed structure and identity. A metabolic process is an *existential mode* of assimilating and becoming one with the environment. Whereas the machine is *having* fuel to go beyond its environment, a metabolism is *merging* with its fuel to attune to its environment. Following Bataille's argument about the curse of excess and expenditure, the metabolism of living processes by necessity produces waste, where pleasure itself is a burst of abundance. However, by being attuned to its environment, in working ecologies, such operation does not pollute, but contributes to the cycle of life around it.

It is also easy to disregard the complexity and interdependence of metabolic processes. Even if the organism is autopoietic, self-organizing, and self-designing, its living functions are contingent on the extensive web of life surrounding it. As pointed out by biologist Lynn Margulis, the whole web of life on our planet is deeply interconnected with myriads of bacteria, living across all our world, in the soil, in rocks and oceans, inside plants, animals, and humans. In all these domains, these tiny organisms help continually regulate the living conditions on Earth; they constitute the chemical feedback system that makes metabolisms at all possible across the biosphere.

> "There is only one immutable truth: No being is purely individual; nothing comprises only itself. Everything is composed of foreign cells, foreign symbionts, foreign thoughts. This makes each life-form less like an individual warrior and more like a tiny universe, tumbling extravagantly through life like the fireflies orbiting one in night. Being alive means participating in permanent community and continually reinventing oneself as part of an immeasurable network of relationships." (Weber 2017: 36)

The motor metaphor may make us think metabolism is by necessity extractive and the engine as something separate from the fuel. This would lead us to believe metabolism feeds on something external that is by necessity diminished, but we must think of metabolism more as a symbiotic process across several spheres of life. Metabolic processes are ingrained in life and interdependent across other domains of life. "A deep part of my self is not myself," Weber (2017: 60) suggests, "My body does not consist of my own specific particles because the matter that makes up my body is constantly changing. The changes in my body physically connect me to all other particles."

So how are we to think of metabolisms when it comes to fashion? What typically distinguishes fashion from garments in general is the energetic lifecycle. The catabolic processes, breaking down ingested compounds to be assimilated, differ between the two. Whereas the confrontation with the elements breaks down the material of clothes, other social and emotional processes break down fashion. Fashion is charged with a social energy. It goes in and out of style, and is dependent on the judgments of others.

Every vista has many metabolic patterns. The life cycles move at different paces, with some garments used over an extended time, while we wear others on just a few occasions. It would be a mistake to think matter necessarily would last longer than desires or ideas. Work-wear may stay longer in circulation than party outfits. The winter wool socks may see fewer hours of use per year than the t-shirts worn almost daily. A suit or a cocktail dress can go in and out of use depending on the season in work or socializing patterns. Some parts of the wardrobe may be activated when friends are in town. Some garments stay long in the closet, awaiting the right occasion, but when that time finally comes, we may have lost our interest, or we realize our proportions have changed. We may easily think clothes last longer than the shifting looks, but the idea of the "little black dress" may have a more permanent presence in our minds than the actual dress stays as part of the wardrobe. In each case, different catabolic processes take place.

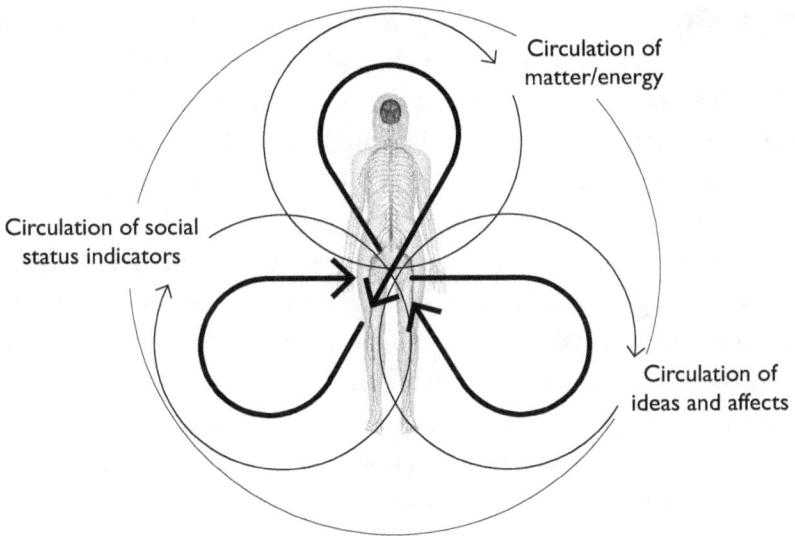

Circulation of matter/energy

Circulation of social status indicators

Circulation of ideas and affects

The metabolism of identity is made up from many interchanging cycles of interconnected substances

When it comes to our body, a plethora of bacteria and micro-organisms that live inside us help in the metabolic process, not least in our gastrointestinal tract. These microbes are the "dark matter" of our inner cosmos, unnoticed to us, but enacting influence on our lives and evolution. They are our cohabitants throughout life, and we could not survive without them. In a similar vein, we must not think that we are the sole consumers of our wardrobe. In the elemental vista, the entropy that breaks down our garments are moth and pests, but also the cigarette burns or clumsy feet of peers. In the end, it is the microbes in the soil or water that will consume the fibers of our garments. Across the relational vistas, social parasites and copycats hunger to feed themselves from the looks of popular peers, a process that quickly breaks down the status of what was thought reserved for the few. In the imaginal vista, self-doubt feeds on our insecurities, like black holes sucking out the faint light that reaches our deep emotional spaces, leaving garments underused.

In its connection to fashion, metabolism spotlights how users engage with and *assimilate fashion into their lives*, through cycles of digestion, use, and excretion. The process happens across all vistas, but may move at a different pace. For example, a pair of sneakers are worn and rubbed away in daily use, but are also consumed and processed as images and status symbols, and being in the "know" about various styles and what is cool at the moment is another form of digestion of their value as desired objects. Like in organic metabolism, this process can be fast or slow, depending on context and efforts. Some types of garments, images, and ideals last longer. Others are quick fixes to a sudden desire, a social occasion, a date, a response to low blood sugar, or a drop in self-esteem. The metabolism points to the circulation of matter and energy, that nothing remains folly stable and permanent. To trace the metabolisms of fashion we must think in several overlapping speeds, rhythms, and motilities.

To make it more straightforward, let's break down the vistas a bit more in detail to highlight their central properties.

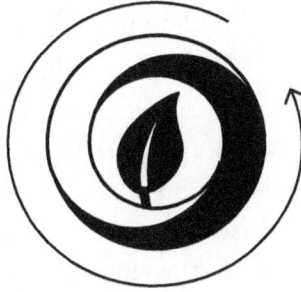

Elemental metabolism

Production: *manufacturing*

Consumption: *use*

Pace: *wear & tear*

Elemental catabolics

- use and material breakdown

- change in user's body proportions & size

Elemental properties of fashion

The metabolism of elemental fashion

The elemental vista is where the idea of clothes as a "second skin" is most apparent: it is what we drape our bodies in, the physical fibers insulating us from the elements. The elemental realm is that of *fashionable goods*, the material aspects of garments and accessories. Here, fashion is incarnated into the physical properties of fibers and production techniques. Most often, it is ready-to-wear. It is a garment or accessory we buy in a store or online. The elemental environment of clothes means how they function with the elements, in the environment of nature.

When it comes to the consumption and circulation of these goods, this is also a realm where we may most obviously have a sense of agency. The user purchases, uses, washes and discards these goods. The direct experience is that we consume fashion, in the form of objects, commodities, or products. In this realm, the success of commodities has exploded over the last decades of globalization. As the price of consumer products has shrunk through globally dispersed production chains, our wardrobes have expanded, and more elemental fashion is in production and on its way to end up in landfills or incinerated.

The metabolism of elemental fashion concerns how material goods circulate in daily life. They are produced, shipped, purchased, shared or rented, and worn, washed, repaired, recycled, and wasted. Garments are bought and worn, but also circulate as hand-me-downs, resold at second-hand and vintage stores, shared via lending libraries and sharing platforms, remade through upcycling and remanufacturing businesses.

Most innovations in the elemental vista deal with biomaterials and other eco-friendly modes of producing garments. Some goods need durable materials, whereas others need ephemeral materials that quickly decompose and break down once their programmed function has reached its full use.

When it comes to the metabolic cycles of energy and matter, it is the users' utilization and wear of these items that "consume" them in the elemental realm. Here, the elements wear down garments; the fabric gets bleached by the sun, the seams ripped by wear and friction, fibers may lose their shape over time, or they degrade over cycles of reuse and remanufacturing, to finally be broken down in the biosphere.

Reflection:

What more examples can you think of describing the metabolism and circulation of elemental fashion?

Relational metabolism
Production: *lifestyles*
Consumption: *image saturation*
Pace: *status/reference inflation*

Relational catabolics
• immersion in lifestyle
• change in relationships and taste

Relational properties of fashion

The metabolism of relational fashion

Fashion is a social phenomenon. It doesn't exist in isolation. It is always relational, enacted between people, in contrast between individuals and groups. By comparing us to others, playing with competition as much as belonging, fashion is a tension and release of anticipation and identification. Fashion is mirrored between people as a social and cultural reality. It appears in informal expectations, aspirations, and the masquerades of social play. In this vista, the focus is on how fashion plays out across social hierarchy and identities, using semiotics and communication, subtle cues, and side looks. It plays out across what we could call the *semiosphere of fashion*, as it concerns how social beings coordinate values and hierarchies through relational behaviors. This is the aspect of the living biosphere in which sign processes operate to modulate feeling and desire.

Again, we must see that as much of a cultural phenomenon we think fashion is, it is grounded in the biology of our feelings and desires to connect, mirror, and compare. As Weber points out;

"Whenever neurobiologists observe that the brain is constantly learning, this therefore means that for as long as we are alive, we are part of a process of mental and bodily growth wherein we interpret encounters and transform ourselves into the history of these encounters. The brain is thereby a reflective organ of the world, comprising primarily relationships. It reflects these relationships by producing relationships within itself, by establishing relationships to the relationships in the world, and by attaching new relationships onto these existing relationships. The brain is an organ that reflects the world by simultaneously making itself into a part of this world." (2017: 42)

Like the nutrients in metabolism becoming part of our body, we assimilate relations into our sense of self. We metabolize energized images to feed ourselves. We watch ourselves being looked at, but it is through the mirroring in the eyes of others we also come to see ourselves. In this way, fashion scholar Shahinda Bari (2020: 53) notes, fashion is a second skin as much as an out-of-body perspective of self-awareness. As we may see different aspects of the self in the many eyes of audience and peers, fashion unfolds a variety of selves, but also all the selves we could have been, ghosts that haunt our wardrobes as much as our dreams, like lost lovers, romanticized and unrealized.

When we consume fashion in this realm, it is in the relational sense. We compare ourselves with peers, presenting an image and performing a persona of who we want to be recognized as *relative to others*. Fashion still takes the form of commodities, but here the process is how we assimilate with them to turn ourselves into commodities on the market of recognition and likability. To use another metaphor, if the elemental realm connoted the physical hardware of garments, the relational is more the social software of fashion.

From a metabolic perspective, fashion is caught in processes of representation, images, and shared desires, in which our energies ebb and flow. Our attention and interests shifts, most often in tune with our peers (even if we seldom acknowledge that). This also means many garments may remain unused in the wardrobe. Sometimes we lose interest after only appearing in it a few times. Other times the right occasions to present the specific relationship the garment offers fails to appear, and a garment may be left untouched so long we almost forgot it was there. That same garment has lost some of its luster, as it no longer stands in relation to the desired connotations we once approved of, but now seems to relate to things past. The relational properties that once energized it have been consumed and drained. What once stood out with an edge now appears bland and lifeless.

Reflection:

Relational fashion takes place in our social life. What examples can you think of how the use of social media manipulates the metabolism of relational fashion?

Imaginal metabolism

Production: *affects/emotions*

Consumption: *identification*

Pace: *updates/social encounters*

Imaginal catabolics

- status updates
- social cues

Imaginal properties of fashion

The metabolism of imaginal fashion

Fashion affects our sense of subjectivity. It ties to our mental states, our innermost domains of feelings and desires. We may claim we don't care much, and dress out of habit. Yet most often, we care enough to be sure of what we like. As opposed to that, we may experience a strong bodily emotion when we assert we would "never wear *that*." On some level, we care, even when we say we don't.

The imaginal vista of fashion connects to our sense of self-knowledge and self-esteem. It is the psychological realm of dress, where trends somehow seep into our minds, affecting how we project ideals onto ourselves and our world. It is also the vista of figures of thought, of fantasies and dreams. It is inhabited by mental models of what is considered positive and negative, pleasure and pain, right and wrong. We may think feeling stays on the inside, but we must recognize it forms our behaviors, expressions, bodies, and senses. "Feeling is never invisible; it takes shape and manifests as form everywhere in nature. Nature can, therefore, be viewed as feeling unfurled, a living reality in front of us and amidst us." (Weber 2016: xiii) Here, we must think of fashion as a mirror that helps shape our inner feelings and selfhood - the imaginal vista as a domain of continuously becoming a living and emotionally engaged subject. Biologist and psychologist Wilhelm Reich offers a compelling image of how our emotions affect the ebb and flow of energies in our bodies;

> "*Fundamentally, emotion is nothing but a plasmatic movement.* Pleasurable stimuli effect an 'emotion' of the protoplasm from the center toward the periphery. Non-pleasurable stimuli, on the other hand, bring about an 'emotion' or, more correctly, 're-motion' of the protoplasm from the periphery toward the center of the organism. These two basic directions of the biophysical plasma current correspond to the two basic affects of the psychic apparatus, pleasure and anxiety." (Reich 1973: 137f)

Reich points out how emotions and re-motions stream through our bodies, making what we usually think of as "merely" feelings and thoughts have real psychosomatic effects. The imaginal is embodied. Neuroscientist Antonio Damasio (2003: 96) points this out,

> "Can one imagine a more distinct body posture than that of the person beaming with pride? What exactly *beams*? The eyes to be sure, wide open, focused and intent on taking on the world; the chin held high; the neck and torso as vertical as they can get; the chest unfearingly filled with air; the steps firm and well planted. These are just some bodily changes we can see."

Like Damasio points to, even if immaterial, imaginal fashion affects our sense of embodiment. How comfortable we are in specific cuts, fabrics, silhouettes, and looks. In the imaginal vista, we play with dress to shape our self-image, our "phantom self" (von Busch & Hwang 2018).

Remember, fashion is social, so the imaginal domain does not merely affect the individual, but is a flow of affects, ripples of moods that spread across populations. Chains of imitation, what sociologist Gabriel Tarde (1903) calls "rays of imitation," intersect, clash and mix into new combinations of ideas, postures, behaviors, and desires. This affects the metabolism in the imaginal vista of fashion, and it becomes even more present through social media. Here, the flow of images and enhanced looks is in an escalating process on its way to saturate our attention. Too little affirmation affects emotions negatively, whereas too much focus on the online presence and success easily leads to burn-out, a tendency social theorist Byung-Chul Han (2015) has framed as the "burnout society."

When we consume fashion in the imaginal realm, its metabolism affects the ebb and flow of self-esteem. On a bad day, with low blood sugar, we crave a boost of energy. It can be a piece of cake or just something new. We consume to lift our mood and boost our self-image with something fresh. The temporary kick helps us feel alive again. But the dopamine quickly drains, and our eyes hunger in search of something new. Or I may feel uncertain before a date or job interview, seeking a new outfit as a boost of self-confidence to calm my nerves.

What can be seen is that the metabolisms of the different vistas are entwined in complex ways, forming patterns of interdependence. A movement in one domain, triggers actions in another. Across consumer culture, we are also encouraged to see growth in one as a symbol for expansion in another. More consumption in the elemental vista connotes symbolic advancement in the relational, which may trigger higher confidence in the imaginal. These patterns is what we need to look into next.

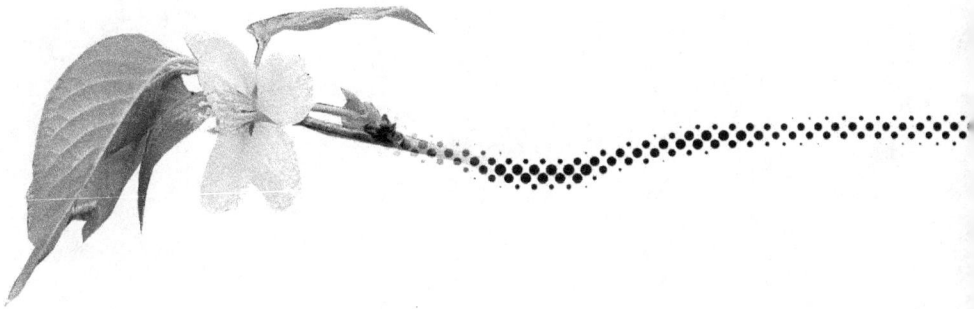

Reflection:

Imaginal fashion is a world of projections and desire. What common tropes or fantasies can you think of that fuel the metabolism of imaginal fashion?

THE METABOLIC BOUNDARIES OF
CIRCULARITY: SHORTFALL & OVERSHOOT

The challenge of sustainability in fashion is manifold. The elemental vista's material pollution is the most visible. Yet, as Guattari points out, we cannot attend to the environment without also changing the social and mental realms. We cannot "fix" nature if we don't change our social practices and thinking. In a similar vein, the challenge of a more sustainable circular fashion is to trace, unpick and remake the energies *exchanged* and in circulation *between* all three vistas, how they interlink, trigger or amplify each other. This is necessary, as we can see similar practices affecting fashion in the three vistas, such as extraction, appropriation, and negligence. We see concentrations of agency and power amongst brands, and we also see similar tendencies in social media, where the attention economy infiltrates the vistas of subjectivity and self-worth. My consumption of goods is connected to peer pressures and my social media presence. These are all connected, and eco-materials won't necessarily fix it.

In the recent decade, there has been a surge of interest in circular business models, which connotes how a business creates, delivers, and captures value. From sustainable and social entrepreneurship to the "triple bottom line," the idea is that business models can effectively attune a business to a specific purpose. This usually means extending conventional business model thinking to a more holistic perspective of value (economic, social, environmental, or "people, profit, and planet") while minimizing waste and extend use-cycles.

In this context, circular business models have emerged to offer more curated and sustainable models for keeping profits attuned to environmental and social commitments. Even if the basic principles of the concept of circularity are not altogether new, the idea has gathered momentum as a critical sustainability catch-all across business, academia, and policymaking. Widespread reports from the Ellen MacArthur Foundation, such as *Vision of a circular economy for fashion* and *Make fashion circular* (2017/2018), have made the ideas easy to digest and apply to business. As fashion emerges as an industry feeding much of the planetary problems, the concept of circular fashion models thus comes as a predictable step to keep the wheels of the industry turning, while mitigating some of the side effects.

However, as has been noted, applying circular design to fashion is not as straightforward as first thought. As a phenomenon essentially connected to change and excess, even reuse and recycling are hard to implement. Even more so, in an intensely competitive market dynamic, complex supply chains and globally distributed stakeholders all push conflicting agendas. While the old mantra of "reduce, reuse, recycle" seems simple enough to understand, applying it to business models and supply chains does not come easy. The aspirations of circularity are usually higher than this bottom line. So far, fashion companies have been slow to adopt circular business models, even as they are promoted to have clear benefits, such as lower costs, higher margins, and improved customer loyalty. The benefits are also widely debated. With global supply chains, the imperative to reduce, reuse and recycle is not as straightforward as it may sound. Sharing may not be local, repairs sent overseas, and recycled materials are a global trade.

While the promise of circular business models is often mentioned, many problems concern how such models can be scaled and if they could be without creating rippling effects that spur unsustainable consequences at other places within the supply chain or organization. Furthermore, holistic models are lacking, and cases are often presented in isolation, with examples of recycling, reselling, sharing, leasing, remanufacturing, while not paying attention to how these cases are embedded into global and cultural contexts. On a general level, too often, the discussion focuses on sustaining the default mode of consuming goods rather than pushing towards a fuller potential of fashion. The prospect of circular models may lie in the curation of combined or hybrid business models, spanning the three vistas. A product can move through several business models throughout its lifecycle, where at various instances, services, experiences, workshops, or events energize its affective motility in tune with the laws of desire.

The utopian potential of circular business models should not be played down. Circular systems thinking can help us attune economies and well-being to the limits of the planet. But there are other troubles also appearing in the imagination of circularity, which concerns the flow of goods and services throughout the economy. These issues become especially concerning when it comes to fashion, as it is based on a continuous flow of styles and expressions. That is, can there be too much or too little flow, too fast or too slow circulation? How does a desire to grow take place within a circular framework? This brings us to another parameter in circularity; how living systems can have a shortfall of energy, or overshoot their boundaries of sustainment. In both cases, metabolic systems are out of balance, failing to support living functions, and can suffer a catastrophic breakdown.

To make this easier to see, a helpful figure of thought is the doughnut model suggested by Kate Raworth. In her visionary book *Doughnut economics* (2017), Raworth puts forward a model through which to find the sweet spot of economic prosperity, between the social

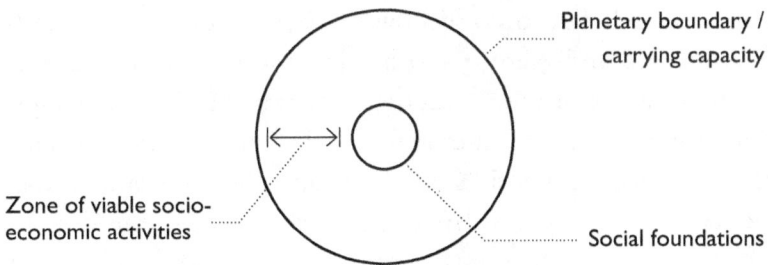

Raworth's model of Doughtnut Economics

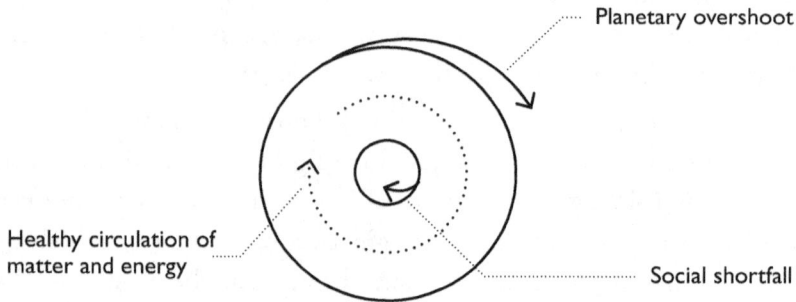

Raworth's model adapted to show circular overshoot and shortfall

foundations, based on the United Nations' Sustainable Development Goals, and the ecological ceilings, the planetary boundaries of the planetary life support systems.

Too little economic activity leads to a shortfall of essential human flourishing, while too much entails a systemic overshoot where the planetary habitability is threatened. Raworth posits that current economic models fail to grasp how to address the shortfall, as large populations are underserved and live in poverty. On the other hand, the programmed quest for perpetual economic growth ignores planetary boundaries and the limits of what our living ecosystems can support. Challenged from both "inside" and "outside" the economic models of society need to stay in balance in the green zone of the "doughnut," serving the fundamental human needs for the broad population while not exceeding the planetary boundaries with excess.

Raworth's model calls to put the economy in service to life. A similar approach is needed as we model the metabolisms of fashion; to make sure fashion works in favor of aliveness.

Not all intensities and speeds of circulation support the metabolism but may instead cause stress to the living functions. For example, too much circulation of matter can lead to saturation and pollution, eventually leading to a poisoning of the system. The evidence of this in consumer societies is abundant. But too little circulation of matter and energy leads to undernourishment, and poverty in human communities. With too intense circulation, nutrients are extracted too fast, or the system grows too quick, overreaching, leaving it fragile. But with too weak circulation, the system grows numb, leaving tissue to die or

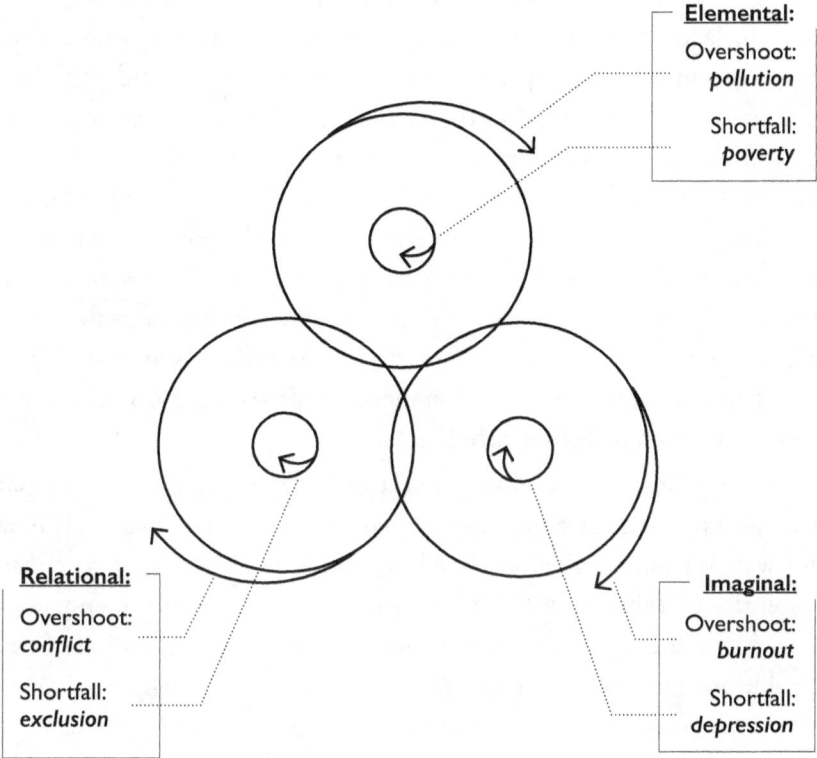

Elemental:
Overshoot:
pollution

Shortfall:
poverty

Relational:
Overshoot:
conflict

Shortfall:
exclusion

Imaginal:
Overshoot:
burnout

Shortfall:
depression

Circular overshoot and shortfall across the three vistas

the system to shrink and whither. With too slow circulation, mobility decreases, and the system stagnates. But with fast circulation, the system reaches fatigue quickly.

We can see that the metabolisms of fashion face similar situations of systemic shortfalls and overshoots. While cheap and accessible fashion reaches increasing populations across the planet, many are still underserved by the potential fashion has for flourishing. Inaccessibility to fashion interferes with the potential of fashion. Current social and relational value systems equate luxury consumption with influence and status. People who are not participating in this game of appearances may be implicitly or explicitly excluded.

But on the other hand, a too intense environment of consumption can lead to increased judgment and social conflict, where peers trigger evermore consumption to keep up and not be considered a "loser." Finally, in the imaginal vista, we may translate consumption habits and affirmation on social media to our sense of self-worth. Here, we may work on our online presence to intensify the flows of attention and likes. Yet, with too little imaginal flow feel depressed as we see everyone else around us succeed and live extraordinary lives, or we may push too hard and burn out as every online friendship becomes an attention exchange. In all these cases, circularity is not a solution in itself, but we need to consider how the energetic flows work across the metabolism of each interconnected vista.

Similarly, just focusing on circularity easily ignores the patterns in which the circular metabolism occurs. In fashion, even if we find ways to make material recycling and remanufacturing with zero waste, the systems in which this takes place still consume enormous amounts of energy in industrial processes and logistics. On top of this, circulation may mean less extraction, but not necessarily less appropriation, less labor exploitation, less willful ignorance, and disregard of best practices. This is also why the three vistas can offer a more holistic view across the domains where fashion connects to social relationships and their connection to self-worth: solving a problem isolated in one of the vistas may not help unpick the systemic pattern.

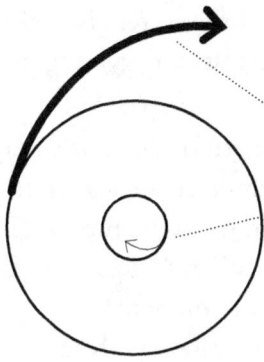

Material circulation:
What happens with too much stuff?
- saturation, poisoning
What happens with too little stuff?
- undernourishment, poverty

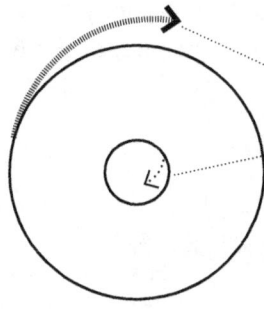

Circulation force:
What happens with too intense circulation?
- exthaust of nutrients/energy
What happens with too weak circulation?
- numbness, extinction

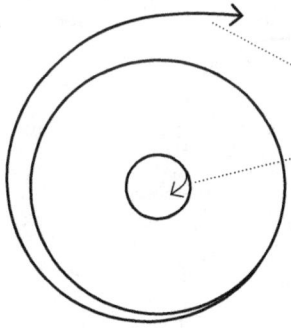

Circulation speed:
What happens with too fast circulation?
- fatigue, enervation
What happens with too slow circulation?
- less mobility, stagnation

It is common knowledge that the default system of fashion is in a continuous metabolic cycle that overshoots the planetary boundaries. What triggers the continuous growth of the system is a self-amplifying feedback-loop interlinking the three vistas, triggering evermore consumption of goods.

The issue resides in the unhealthy pattern that has emerged, as already noted by Guattari, between the three ecologies, or the three vistas. As my subjective well-being is tied to my consumption, in order to feel good about myself (in my mental ecology) I feel a need to buy more stuff. The new acquisitions (in the environmental ecology) trigger new social competition as the social relations with my peers are affected, thus triggering more purchases across the social ecology. The social hierarchies are thus affected, again threatening to undermine my self-esteem, thus I need to bolster my emotions by again buying more items. Consumption increases, and the carrying capacity of each vista is overshot, leading to increased pollution everywhere; in the material, social and mental domains.

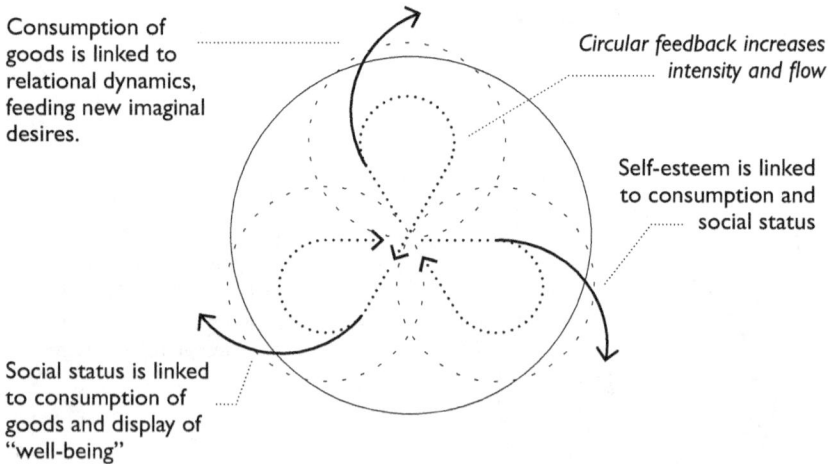

Consumption of goods is linked to relational dynamics, feeding new imaginal desires.

Circular feedback increases intensity and flow

Self-esteem is linked to consumption and social status

Social status is linked to consumption of goods and display of "well-being"

Current circular dynamics, linked across the three vistas, trigger continuous overshoot of the carrying capacity.

The opposite dynamics can also take place, where a feedback cycle of shortfall leads to unmet needs in each and every vista. Material poverty can lead to social exclusion, which in turn brings along bad self-esteem and depression. As pointed out in economist Manfred Max-Neef's taxonomy of Fundamental human needs, it is not a chicken and egg situation; the negative cycle can emerge from any of the vistas and touch off a downward spiral.

These self-sustaining dynamics may take different shape, and certainly differ across cultures and situations, but they also share many traits. If we are to address sustainability in fashion, they are essential cycles that form a pattern that needs to be addressed and changed. Shifting focus towards skills, capabilities and engagement may be one way, and we will discuss this more in detail as we move along.

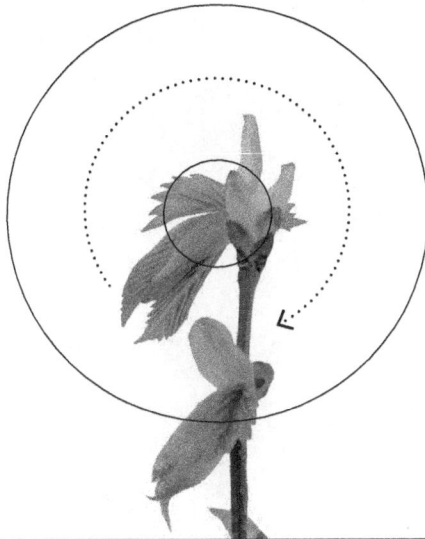

Reflection:

Can you think of other examples of circulation overshoot or shortfall? What has been your own experiences?

DEPTHS OF ENGAGEMENT AND
VITAL FASHION-ABILITIES

When we consume fashion, in almost all cases we buy *fashionable stuff*. Fashionable things are things we acquire, buy, possess, consume and waste. Fashion is associated with *having*. But if fashion is a living energy, a metabolism that helps assimilate us into the living environment of the now, then it may be more beneficial for us to think of fashion as an ability, a fashion-*ability*. We can be fashionable; it is about *being*, rather than having. Just like metabolism is an existential mode, we must think of how we assimilate with fashion-abilities as an *existential process*.

Fashion-abilities modulate our living experience with fashion. This means first and foremost acknowledging the user's agency in the emergence of the embodied feeling of fashion. Fashionable goods offer the wearer an agency of fashion through appearance, by dressing in a specific stylish garment. It gives the wearer an aura of being fashionable by a process similar to osmosis. Fashion-ability, on the other hand, puts the conditions of the user at the center, as the metabolic process sets the living processes and feelings as the point of gravity. Fashion-abilities are about more agency, more control, more capabilities shared with users in order to cultivate their participatory abilities.

To get there, the interaction between designer and users cannot stay at the surface of things, or by calling the consumer to only passively purchase ready-made products, services, and experiences. Users must be offered some of the agency we keep reserved for the "insiders" of the industry. Users must be invited deeper into the processes of production around fashion, into a *depth of engagement*.

Engagement may be a word with a multitude of confusing or contradictory connotations. But what I wish to stress is how it ties into the *intensification* of aliveness. Engagement opens a more comprehensive interface between the parts meeting, allowing for more emotional commitment, communication, and coordination between meaning and behavior. When it comes to intensity, this does not necessarily need to mean excitement and passion, but could also take place in the very human ability of contemplation and reflection over aliveness - in the "gardening work" of becoming.

As pointed out before, each of the three vistas translates to a domain or reality of fashion. In each vista, fashion helps the user experience a landscape of sensibility, touch, and be in contact with a particular aspect of reality. Fashion is attuned to each vista's environment and works as a sensory prosthetic for our senses. And as a sensory organ, it needs to be trained to adjust to its environment. This sensory ability is what we could call the *depth of engagement*.

A depth of engagement signifies how a user can attune to a vista of fashion, become literate to read the environment and gain capabilities to inhabit and influence this vista in ways that enhance the user's agency. This is a way of rethinking a retail space to become something more than racks of ready-to-wear, but a space that deepens a user's sensibility for fashion's potential for triggering aliveness. Engagement means more than mere activation. As with the metabolism, it means a deeper *assimilation of vitality*. Vitality is not a fuel that burns in my engine, but it becomes part of my organism; I grow and feel with it, mirroring my being in my living environment.

A depth of engagement goes beyond default fashion, breaks with the distinction between producer and consumer, or between designer and user. Design and production are not kept separate and obscure or far removed from users. Instead, there is a continuum between the user and designer, where the user is invited to take steps to engage deeper with fashion-abilities. It goes beyond the shallow notion of users simply buying, sharing, or repairing the ready-to-wear goods offered to them. *With engagement, depth becomes growth.*

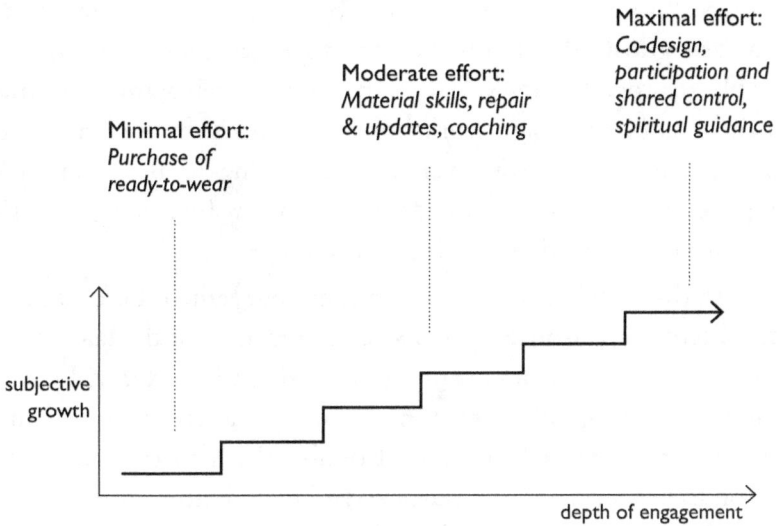

Minimal effort:
*Purchase of
ready-to-wear*

Moderate effort:
*Material skills, repair
& updates, coaching*

Maximal effort:
*Co-design,
participation and
shared control,
spiritual guidance*

subjective
growth

depth of engagement

*The depth of engagement offers a path towards vertical growth, in
skills and in relational and affective capabilities*

In the elemental vista, this may mean getting a deeper understanding of how material qualities and production techniques influence the design and the skills of caring for a garment or repairing it. For
a retail space, this may mean inviting the user to enter an environment
furnished with sewing machines and equipment for repairs and remanufacturing, spare parts, and modular elements ready for redesign. Here,
the depth means an increasing material engagement with garments,
gaining agency to affect the elemental vistas of one's wardrobe.

In the relational vista, a depth of engagement is a space of togetherness. Here, fashion is a tool for self-expression and individuality
as much as a point of gravity for peers to gather around. Here, the social elements of co-design and production come to the forefront. Think
of the depth as starting from simply social consumption, or shopping
with friends, to more wholehearted celebrations of togetherness and

friendship. It can be shared events, from guided tours, lectures, and workshops, to more social events and bonding, using the energies of fashion as a gravity that holds the parts together. From just a space to shoot photos together for social media to more celebratory masquerades and events, co-design workshops with the in-house team in the design studio to take-over events by emerging local communities. Along the axis of engagement, depth means an increasing attention and agency in the relational realm of fashion.

In the imaginal vista, the depth of engagement becomes more urgent. Here, the purpose is to raise consciousness of the background drives and motivations of consumption. Fashion is traditionally based on taking advantage of a consumer's lousy self-esteem to sell more goods to temporarily fill the void of doubt. With a depth of engagement, on the other hand, the purpose will be to better serve the user's needs for growth and increased self-knowledge and encouragement to challenge the customary. Here, a depth of engagement can mean a process of healing rather than profiting from a consumer's self-doubt. But it can also be much more than that; a summons to flourish.

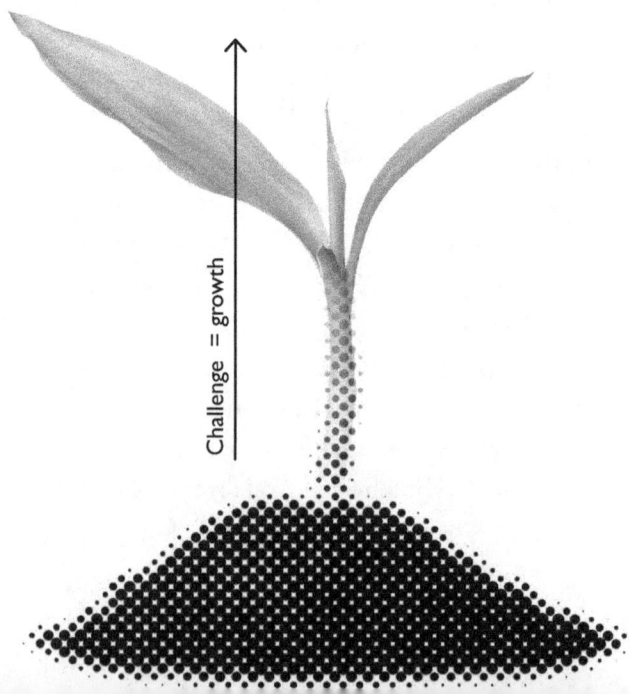

Challenge = growth

While healing may sound wholesome and good, flourishing demands a challenge, a process of overcoming, not a tranquil stagnant state of being. A sprout in spring awakes from winter's hibernation, breaks out from its shell, thrusting upwards towards the sun, against gravity and the elements. Flourishing means more than just being wholesome, authentic, and healthy - it means thriving in the face of a challenge. The flourishing of fashion-abilities sets out on a similar journey, to transgress the default settings of habits to attune to the laws of desire; to grow, to feel, to mirror.

To draw parallels to the ideas of philosopher Peter Sloterdijk's *You must change your life* (2013), flourishing is a "lifting of the soul," and is partly fuelled by *thymotic* (pride- and ambition-based) as well as *erotic* (greed- and libido-based) energies. There is a direction on the process of self-design, on the "auto-plastic journey," and it travels along an inner vertical axis of cultural values. Like the sprout challenging gravity, flourishing means to aspire for what we culturally and individually consider "higher" than what is merely customary or profane: an extension of abilities towards our desires.

> "Vitality, understood both somatically and mentally, is itself the medium that contains a gradient between more and less. It, therefore, contains the vertical component that guides ascent within itself" (Sloterdijk 2013: 39).

A depth of engagement means an aspiration for vitality and verticality. Energetic, playful, but remains an ascent. This is why the ladder of deeper engagement leads upwards; towards the potentials of self-design. Existentially, it is a process that explores higher possibilities of being human, and aspires for a more god-like agency to shape one's life, utilizing appearances and the techniques of *being* with clothes. When fashion works, we feel it as an auto-poiesis that grows our human potential.

Think of fashion-abilities as a form of exercise equipment. We use them in what Sloterdijk calls the "practice of life," the struggle to improve, grow, and seek that which one considers higher. Fashion is a masquerade that does not bring us further from each other, but closer. And by being a "deep play," it is a practice that is animated by the heights, while it can help us practice to be closer to our vertical and aspirational selves.

Fashion-abilities are thus not merely skills or external capabilities. While they may involve skills in sewing and repair, knowledge of materials and techniques, sensibility for textures and qualities, fashion-abilities are inner tools, used in the perfection of one's life journey, practicing to *utilize the potentials of fashion* to the fullest. Along with Sloterdijk's argument, we can place fashion as a method or interface to practice an ideal of living, not merely appearing vain, buying access to goods we hope will elevate us by osmosis. To flourish with fashion means to journey upwards, growing, feeling, and mirroring one's cosmic status through auto-plastic practices of self-design.

So we are approaching the end of this journey together, and you may ask, what is to be done? To start with, if we are serious about the ideals we strive for in making fashion more sustainable, the question must become how we can offer fashion users a wider interface towards practicing the vital life. The cultivation of fashion-abilities helps support users in their aspirations towards self-improvement. Fashionable goods always risk becoming mere tokens and need extensive circulation and updates, while fashion-abilities can grow in depth and intensity. As a form of ecological design intelligence, fashion-abilities help support the users in their struggles to practice their ideals for living.

This situates fashion with the cultivation of skills and spiritual practices, engagements with life in which we try to live up to inner held beliefs and paths towards perfection. In such a setting, the bottom line is offering support to make lasting change, starting to improve my life from the wardrobe and out; care services and instructions, spare parts, updates, but also a mutual sense of commitment and techniques by which I can grow, feel, and ascend. In this case, we can embrace fashion as part of a life journey, an ongoing endeavor aiming for what we hold as supreme nobility of the soul. To not only consume fashionable goods, but to *live fashion-ably*. And such integrity can also be available to those with fewer means in supporting care and repair, inviting users to practice the values a brand suggests it embraces. We all need help to become masters of the conditions of our existence, beyond buying the future on discount.

We must think of fashion a play of excess. It is an existential mode for exploring the world. With fashion, we examine meanings and boundaries, what works and what doesn't work, through practical experience and aesthetic experimentation. It involves many layers of our selves, and each is challenged to grow; through physical, cognitive, and emotional journeys propelled by the laws of desire. As a path of exploration, ascend and transformation, our play with fashion is intimately and intricately connected with our elemental and relational worlds, but even more so with abilities of creativity, daring, boldness, and risk-taking. It is a play that opens us to the world, to the affects of our peers, to sensing the world of togetherness.

Fashion cannot be experienced in isolation; it is a social phenomenon. It may help us practice a life of mutualism and commitment. The challenge is to make sure those who need fashion-abilities the most will also be able to access and cultivate them to practice aliveness together.

"Like poetry, like love, like the rapt and agonizing commitment to a collective concern, like a stirring idea or a humorous insight, aliveness is something that increases when we share it." (Weber 2017: 189)

WORKBOOK

Now when we have gotten a basic grasp on the metabolic cycles of circularity, we can start the real work. The task ahead is to imagine new *patterns* of metabolisms that work across the three vistas. Current economic models do not help us see interconnected circular vistas, and especially not how they can support more sustainable patterns that also facilitate a flourishing of aliveness.

Our task is to tie together and create synergies between the vistas that animate fashion in new ways, and that helps foster fashionabilities. Using a depth of engagement, the visionary work involves tracing patterns where material goods become more energized through the relational and imaginal domains. Our purpose is to make the circular processes more vital, and help trigger new exploration, growth, and aliveness.

The diagrams in the coming pages are tools by which to start thinking around how such connections may look. They are tools with which to develop the ecological design intelligence needed to help the passions and desires of fashion thrive, while keeping the experience of excess within the carrying capacities of the vistas.

Please observe, these diagrams are points of departure. They are material to work from. Pushing fashion towards deeper flourishing is a collective endeavor of imagination and visionary work.

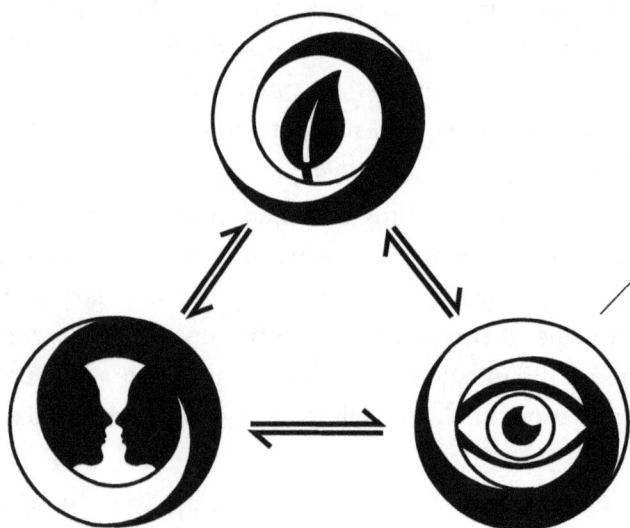

Elemental

Imaginal

Relational

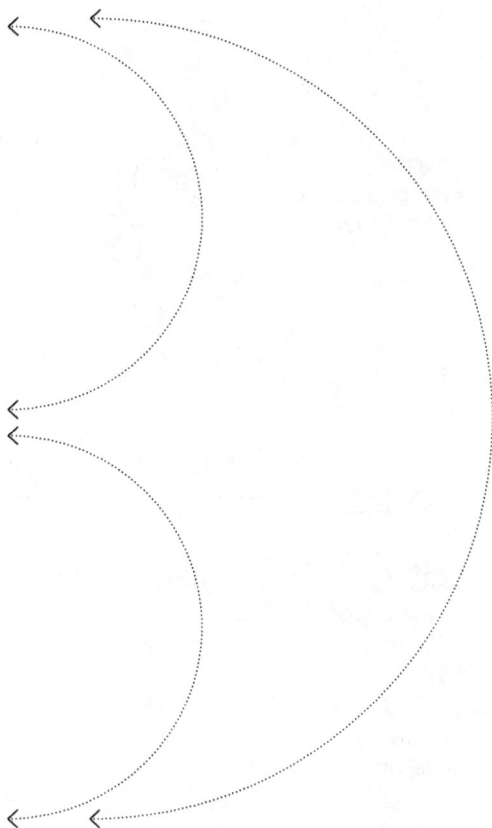

(+) **EXAMPLE OF A METABOLIC PATTERN**

This spread gives the key of how to map and work on expanding a metabolic cycle in a vista by animating it with feedback from another vistas.

type of practice

systemic boundary

Challenges:
Issues and problems apparent in the cycle

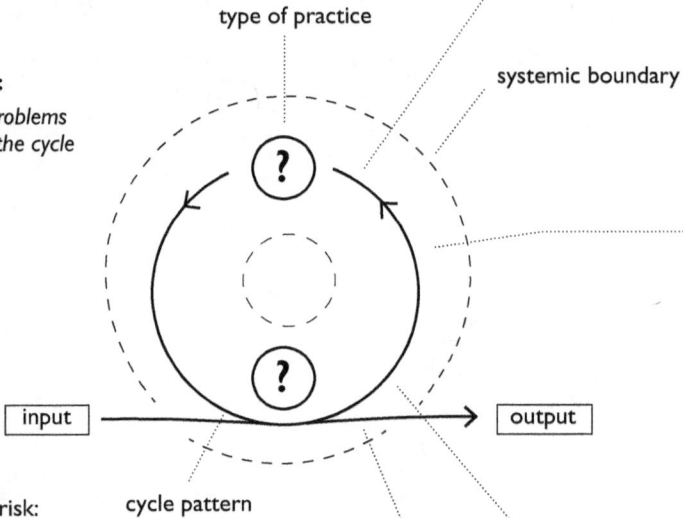

?

?

input

output

Overshoot risk:
Tendency to exceed environmental boundaries

cycle pattern

Shortfall risk:
Tendency towards circular deficit

Guiding questions:

Here you will find notes and questions to help guide the development of the pattern.

Force of animation from another vista:

- *What practice from another vista that can help animate the sense of flourishing in this pattern?*

Force of animation from another vista:

- *What practice from another vista that can help animate the sense of flourishing in this pattern?*

Vitality/growth:

- *What is the quality of flourishing this pattern can help cultivate?*

Vision fashion-*ability*:

- *How can the depth of engagement be experienced?*
- *What kind of fashion-abilities can be fostered?*

DEADSTOCK REDESIGN

Garments are made from surplus or recycled materials is a common strategy to lower the environmental footprint in production.

Challenges:

Manufacturing:
May not be fair labor

Material:
Overstock quality

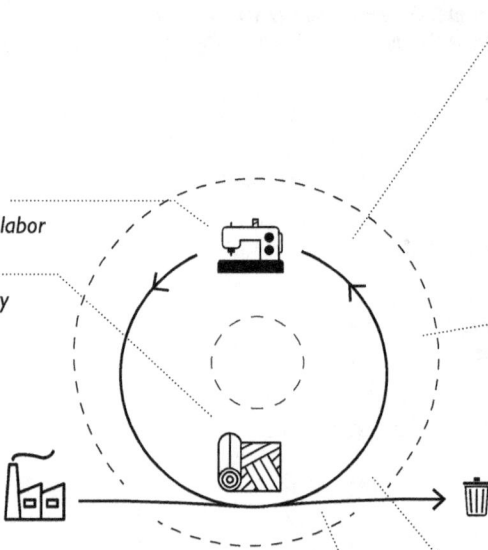

Overshoot risk:
Too much goods produced and circulated

Shortfall risk:
Deadstock stays dead

Guiding questions:

- *Using deadstock for new collections gets more common, yet beyond the hype little has changed. Zero waste is another. Can these techniques be more engaging, transparent, or playful?*

Animation from relational vista:

Animation from imaginal vista:

Vitality/growth:

Vision fashion-*ability*:

RECOMMERCE

Recommerce is the resale circulation of previously owned garments, where an item change owner several times across its journey.

Challenges:

Resale value:
*Requires curation
to maintain value*

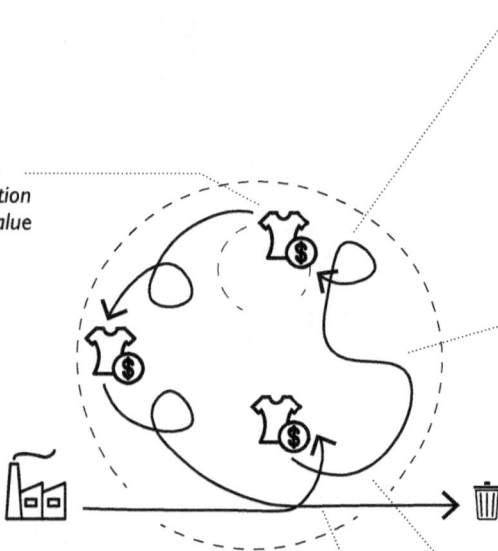

Overshoot risk:
*Too many items
in circulation*

Shortfall risk:
*Unsold items
become deadstock*

Guiding questions:
- *Even bland everyday things can have their value and meaning recharged by passing through processes of validation where new desire is projected onto them (think of TV show Antiques Roadshow). What provenance contributes to the value of fashion, and how can such stories be told, and by whom?*

Animation from relational vista:

Animation from imaginal vista:

Vitality/growth:

Vision fashion-*ability*:

RENTAL

Rental systems are basically fashion libraries. Garments are not owned by the user but leased for an individual occasion or through monthly subscriptions.

Challenges:

Care:
Users may become less caring

Attachment:
Use may not last long enough to become attached

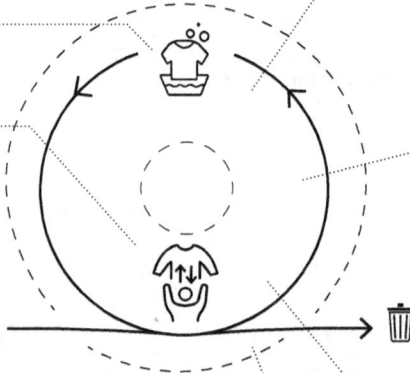

Overshoot risk:
Increasing demand for new rental items

Shortfall risk:
Inaccessible or unrented items

Guiding questions:
*   *Rental offers fresh looks when needed, but queuing for the premiere builds an anticipation that is hard to replicate going to the library. How can rental services be more engaging, or foster a sense of growth?*

Animation from relational vista:

Animation from imaginal vista:

Vitality/growth:

Vision fashion-*ability*:

SWAP & REPAIR

Repairs and swapping of garments are services for mending and updating existing garments to keep them in circulation.

Challenges:

Remake/remanufacture:
Requires energy and labor

Repair:
Overall qulity is compromised with each repair

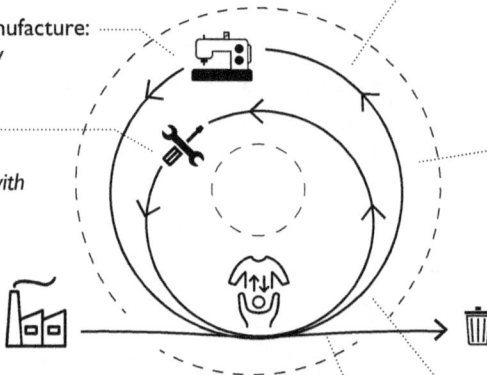

Overshoot risk:
Too much circulation and aquisition

Shortfall risk:
Too few participants, too few exchanges

Guiding questions:
*   *A challenge for repairs and swaps is making the experience special and transformative. Old things promise less than new. Co-design, skillshare, engagement and curation can help reanimate repaired garments. Can users have a say in how things are swapped, updated and repaired?*

Animation from relational vista:

Animation from imaginal vista:

Vitality/growth:

Vision fashion-*ability*:

BIO-MATERIALS

Next generation biodegradable materials are plant-based alternatives to replace oil-based synthetics. These are farmed and produced organically and can be broken down in the compost.

Challenges:

Agriculture:
Scale of current consumption

Industry:
Adjacent industries and systems still unsustainable

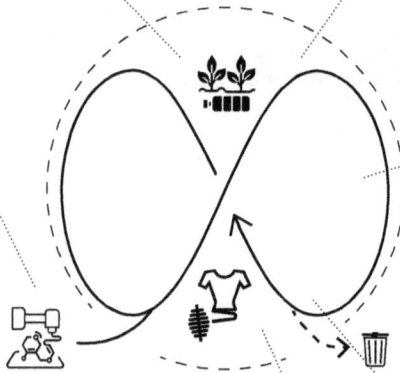

Overshoot risk:
Less pollution becomes incentive to increase scale

Shortfall risk:
Does not reach populations who need them

Guiding questions:

* *Bio-materials seem like the silver bullet for making default fashion sustainable, yet it just patches up the current system. How can bio-materials be used for more utopian purposes? How can users partake and come in closer proximity to fashion-abilities with bio-materials?*

Animation from relational vista:

Animation from imaginal vista:

Vitality/growth:

Vision fashion-*ability*:

ONE-FOR-ONE

While not necessarily circular, for every product sold, the company donates a copy or equivalent item to an underserved community, or contributes to an environmental project.

Challenges:

Recipients:
Target community needs more urgent issues addressed.

Gifts:
Products can have more purpose

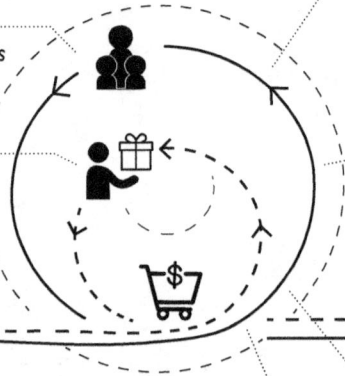

Overshoot risk:
Doubles waste

Shortfall risk:
No purchase, no gift

Guiding questions:

- *A more relation-based engagement with the recipient community can help foster commitment. Can the gifts keep moving so one-for-one gifts go both ways? Can the recipient community have a say in the design and operation of the system? Can the community help the consumer, instead of the other way around?*

Animation from relational vista:

Animation from imaginal vista:

Vitality/growth:

Vision fashion-*ability*:

WARDROBE MINIMALISM

The wardrobe minimalist rethinks the use of our closet inventory depending on our social relations, cutting down and circulating the most useful and fulfilling pieces.

Challenges:

Social standards: *Media and peers treat consumption as the norm*

Social mobility: *Minimal wardrobe decreases social mobility*

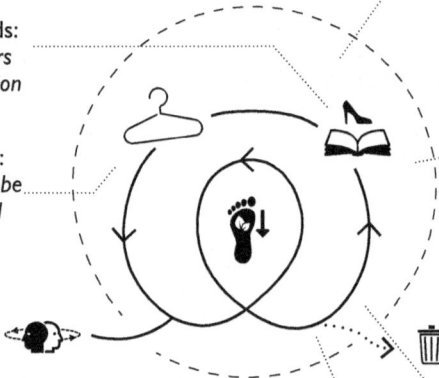

Overshoot risk: *Who can afford to be a minimalist?*

Shortfall risk: *Serves as a cover for conserving poverty and exclusion*

Guiding questions:

- *Minimalism is a seductive approach to a cluttered consumer society where hoarding stands in the way to more consumption. How can a minimal wardrobe best support social mobility and the laws of desire? What kind of engagements can replace new purchases and energize garments that are used habitually? What rituals can support popular minimalism?*

Animation from elemental vista:

Animation from imaginal vista:

Vitality/growth:

Vision fashion-*ability*:

SOCIAL ENTERPRISE

Social enterprise supports marginalized communities with financial and educational resources, striving to maximize social impact through more products or services sold.

Challenges:

Economics:
Replicates colonial economic models

Social capital:
Exploits suffering while maintaining status quo

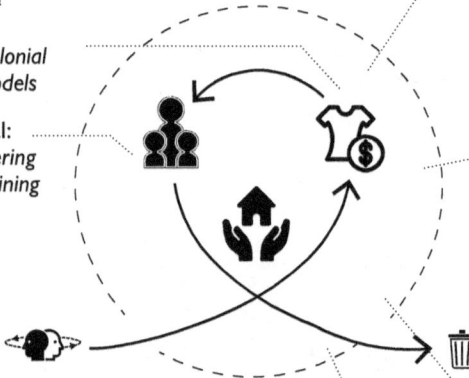

Overshoot risk:
Success increases competition and social conflict

Shortfall risk:
Legitimizes status quo

Guiding questions:
*   *Social enterprise strives to siphon off some profits to do good. A limitation is that it is often tied to sales; the more items sold, the better. It increases pollution, and also limits the social good to industrial production. A competitive global market does not help. What other types of engagements can shift the focus from products?*

Animation from elemental vista:

Animation from imaginal vista:

Vitality/growth:

Vision fashion-*ability*:

JUSTICE ADVOCACY

Justice advocacy utilizes fashion as a tool to advocate for political issues, highlighting societal imbalances and communities that are not represented in society.

Challenges:

Awareness:
Mistaking awareness with social change

Continuity:
Institutional issues take time to address

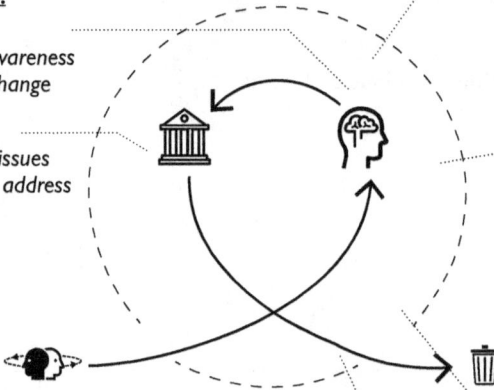

Overshoot risk:
Inflation in struggles

Shortfall risk:
Issue ignored

Guiding questions:
- *How can a social issue be addressed through fashion in more way than as an accessory or slogan? Can a depth of engagement go beyond awareness raising to mobilize commitment and community groups, train participants, practice local and global change, and create more equitable relations?*

Animation from elemental vista:

Animation from imaginal vista:

Vitality/growth:

Vision fashion-*ability*:

COOP ORGANIZING

The coop emphasises and activates commons, structured as a worker cooperative of shared ownership, and is organized around cooperative principles and values.

Challenges:

Larger picture:
A focus on products can fail the larger social vision

Community:
The coop can come to exclude new members

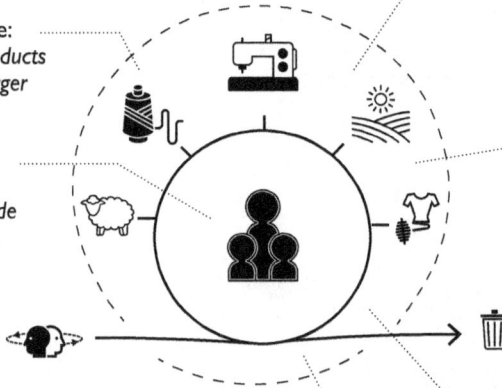

Overshoot risk:
Too many members can become alienating

Shortfall risk:
Dysfunction and stagnation

Guiding questions:

• *The myth of the individual genious designer and creator aligns well with a centralized and hierachical organization. More collective forms of ownership and decisionmaking challenges this picture for a more equitable working community. How can the cooperative vision also inform design, production, media, sales, and user engagement? How can everyone grow together?*

Animation from elemental vista:

Animation from imaginal vista:

Vitality/growth:

Vision fashion-*ability*:

SHOPPING RECOVERY

Under compulsive consumerism, one may need to examine and alter one's shopping patterns, and practice with more balanced set of fashion practices.

Challenges:

Business models:
Continuous growth limits visions of degrowth fashion

Homo economicus:
Thinking subjectivity beyond the profit-maximizing individual

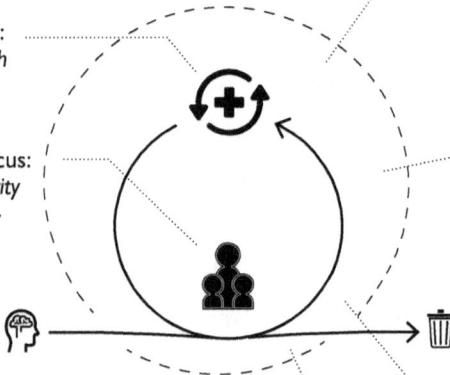

Overshoot risk:
Seeing shopping as normative behavior

Shortfall risk:
Punishing the poor for their desire

Guiding questions:

- *As consumption is a standard fashion practice, it can be challenging to stand outside. Can brands use engagement to decrease consumption? What more imaginative and visionary practices can replace shopping? What regenerative desires can complement and ultimately replace the craving for new stuff?*

Animation from elemental vista:

Animation from relational vista:

Vitality/growth:

Vision fashion-*ability*:

FASHION THERAPY

Modelled after clinical practice, dressing practices are used for therapy geared towards dealing with physical and emotional insecurities, improving mental health and self-esteem.

Challenges:

Beyond consumption:
Not "retail therapy," but dealing with underlying issues

Accessibility:
The most needy are often left out

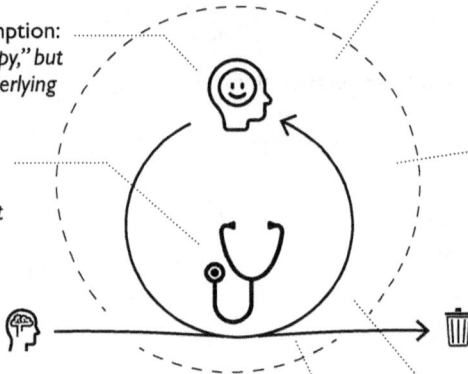

Overshoot risk:
Increases baseline for success and well-being

Shortfall risk:
Ignores systemic issues

Guiding questions:

- *Fashion thrives under bad self-esteem, a brand wants addicted consumers. How can fashion be organized around practices of healing? What kind of engagements could a brand offer that would transcend products and help the user grow as a more thriving and holistic being?*

Animation from elemental vista:

Animation from relational vista:

Vitality/growth:

Vision fashion-*ability*:

EMPATHY STYLING

A "deep" styling that guides a life transition, offing direction through the wardrobe and facilitates new fashion practices.

Challenges:

Norms:
Working with or beyond normative looks

Consumption:
Not making transition dependent on a new wardrobe

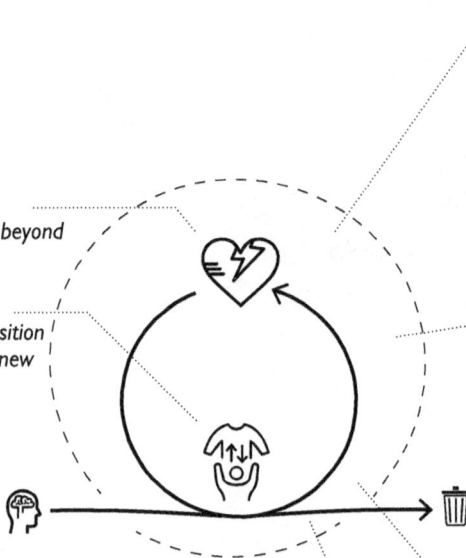

Overshoot risk:
Increasing norm for what is acceptable

Shortfall risk:
Exclusion/depression

Guiding questions:

- *Styling connotes shallowness and not deeper change. What kind of practices can challenge this misunderstanding? A change of appearances comes with rites of passage, breakups and coming-out How can designers and stylists support and facilitate more deep, daring and transformative used of fashion for those who so desire?*

Animation from elemental vista:

Animation from relational vista:

Vitality/growth:

Vision fashion-*ability*:

FASHION SPIRITUAL COACHING

Fashion as a path for spiritual development, with design of rituals and inner practices to ascend and transcend the habitual.

Challenges:

Happiness:
Sets standards for what is a good life and a good person.

Quackery:
Fraudsters using victims

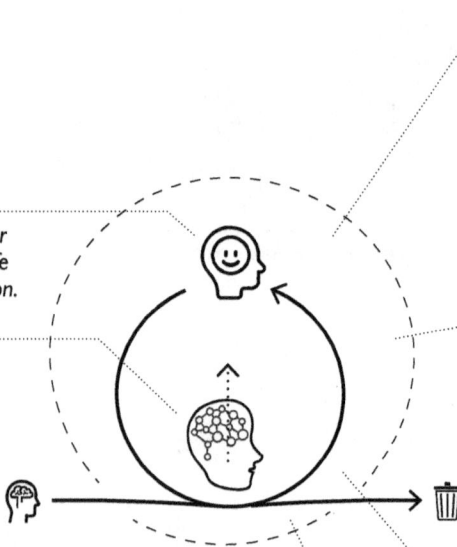

Overshoot risk:
Fresh cults

Shortfall risk:
Does not address underlying issues

Guiding questions:

- *As long as fashion is treated as merely shallow, we fail to see its potential for growth. What can fashion designers learn from spiritual practices that take the inner life of subjects seriously? What rituals and practices can users be engaged in that help them seek, grown, ascend and feel beyond the consumption of goods?*

Animation from elemental vista:

Animation from relational vista:

Vitality/growth:

Vision fashion-*ability*:

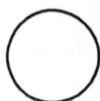

Clean worksheet

Example

Challenges:

input

output

Overshoot risk:

Shortfall risk:

Guiding questions:

Force of animation:

Force of animation:

Vitality/growth:

Vision fashion-ability:

References

Bari, Shahinda (2020) *Dressed: a philosophy of clothes*, New York: Hachette.

Barthes, Roland (1983) *The fashion system*, Berkeley: University of California Press.

Bateson, Gregory (1977) *Steps to an ecology of mind*, New York: Ballantine Books.

Bataille, Georges (1991) *The accursed share: an essay on general economy*, New York: Zone books.

Berry, Wendel (1981) "Solving the pattern," in *The gift of good land*, San Francisco: North Point Press.

Biomimicry Institute (2020) *The nature of fashion: moving towards a regenerative system*, Missoula: The Biomimicry Institute (available at: https://biomimicry.org/thenatureoffashion/)

de Botton, Alain (2012) *How to think more about sex*, London: Macmillan.

von Busch, Otto (2018) *Vital vogue: a biosocial perspective on fashion*, New York: Self-Passage.

von Busch, Otto & Date Hwang (2018) *Feeling fashion: the embodied gamble of our social skin*, New York: SelfPassage.

Capra, Fritjof (2005) "How nature sustains the web of life," in Michal Stone & Zenobia Barlow (eds) *Ecological literacy: educating our children for a sustainable world*, San Francisco: Sierra Club Books.

Earley, Rebecca (2019) *Shirt stories*, University of the Arts London Professional Platform, available at: https://issuu.com/ualresearch/docs/shirt.s__digital_hr

Ehrenfeld, John & Andrew Hoffman (2013) *Flourishing: a frank conversation about sustainability*, Stanford: Stanford University Press.

Fletcher, Kate (2018) *Pocket guide to fashion ecology*, available at; www.fashionecolgies.org.

Fletcher, Kate & Lynda Grose (2012) *Fashion & sustainability: design for change*, London: Laurence King.

Fletcher, Kate & Mathilda Tham (2004) "Clothing rhythms" in Ed van Hinte (ed) *Eternally yours: time in design, product, value, sustenance*, Rotterdam: 010 publishers.

Fletcher, Kate & Mathilda Tham (2019) *Earth logic*, London: JJ Charitable Trust.

Global Fashion Agenda (2021) "7 Things You As A Can Do As A Citizen To Contribute To Circular Fashion," published February 12, 2021, at www.globalfashionagenda.com

Grosz, Elisabeth (2008) *Chaos, territory, art: Deleuze and the framing of the earth*, New York: Columbia University Press.

Guattari, Felix (2000) *The three ecologies*, London: Athlone Press.

Han, Byung-Chul (2015) *The burnout society*, Stanford: Stanford University Press.

Lipovetsky, Gilles (1994) *The empire of fashion: dressing modern democracy*, Princeton: Princeton University Press.

Maturana, Humberto & Francisco Varela (1980) *Autopoiesis and cognition: The realization of the living*. Dordecht: D. Reidel Publishing.

Miller, Joshua (2005) "Fashion and democratic relationships," *Polity*, 37(1): pp. 3-23.

Orr, David (1994) *Earth in mind: on education, environment, and the human prospect*, Covelo: Island Press.

Orr, David (2002) *The nature of design*, Oxford: Oxford University Press.

Raworth, Kate (2017) *Doughnut economics: seven ways to think like a 21st-century economist*, London: Random House.

Reich, Wilhelm (1973) *Selected writings: an introduction to orgonomy*, New York: Farrar, Straus and Giroux.

Sloterdijk, Peter (2013) *You must change your life*, Cambridge: Polity.

Tarde, Gabriel (1903) *The laws of imitation*, New York: Henry Holt.

Weber, Andreas (2016) *The biology of wonder*, Gabriola Island: New Society.

Weber, Andreas (2017) *Matter & desire: an erotic ecology*, White River Junction: Chelsea Green.

www.ingramcontent.com/pod-product-compliance
Lightning Source LLC
Chambersburg PA
CBHW021129020426
42331CB00005B/680